FLOYD CLYMER'S MOTORCYCLIST'S LIBRARY

The Second Book of the
BSA TWINS

Riding and Practical Maintenance Instructions for Owners of all 1962–9 A50 and A65 Type O.H.V. Vertical Twins with Unit Construction of Engine and Gearbox

A. G. Lupton, C.Eng., M.I.Mech.E.

ANNOUNCEMENT

By special arrangement with the original publishers of this book, Sir Isaac Pitman & Son, Ltd., of London, England, we have secured the exclusive publishing rights for this book, as well as all others in THE MOTORCYCLIST'S LIBRARY.

Included in THE MOTORCYCLIST'S LIBRARY are complete instruction manuals covering the care and operation of respective motorcycles and engines; valuable data on speed tuning, and thrilling accounts of motorcycle race events. See listing of available titles elsewhere in this edition.

We consider it a privilege to be able to offer so many fine titles to our customers.

FLOYD CLYMER
Publisher of Books Pertaining to Automobiles and Motorcycles

2125 W. PICO ST.   LOS ANGELES 6, CALIF.

INTRODUCTION

Welcome to the world of digital publishing ~ the book you now hold in your hand, while unchanged from the original edition, was printed using the latest state of the art digital technology. The advent of print-on-demand has forever changed the publishing process, never has information been so accessible and it is our hope that this book serves your informational needs for years to come. If this is your first exposure to digital publishing, we hope that you are pleased with the results. Many more titles of interest to the classic automobile and motorcycle enthusiast, collector and restorer are available via our website at www.VelocePress.com. We hope that you find this title as interesting as we do.

NOTE FROM THE PUBLISHER

The information presented is true and complete to the best of our knowledge. All recommendations are made without any guarantees on the part of the author or the publisher, who also disclaim all liability incurred with the use of this information.

TRADEMARKS

We recognize that some words, model names and designations, for example, mentioned herein are the property of the trademark holder. We use them for identification purposes only. This is not an official publication.

INFORMATION ON THE USE OF THIS PUBLICATION

This manual is an invaluable resource for the classic motorcycle enthusiast and a "must have" for owners interested in performing their own maintenance. However, in today's information age we are constantly subject to changes in common practice, new technology, availability of improved materials and increased awareness of chemical toxicity. As such, it is advised that the user consult with an experienced professional prior to undertaking any procedure described herein. While every care has been taken to ensure correctness of information, it is obviously not possible to guarantee complete freedom from errors or omissions or to accept liability arising from such errors or omissions. Therefore, any individual that uses the information contained within, or elects to perform or participate in do-it-yourself repairs or modifications acknowledges that there is a risk factor involved and that the publisher or its associates cannot be held responsible for personal injury or property damage resulting from the use of the information or the outcome of such procedures.

WARNING!

One final word of advice, this publication is intended to be used as a reference guide, and when in doubt the reader should consult with a qualified technician.

Preface

An extremely popular range of B.S.A. A7 and A10 type vertical twins was manufactured by B.S.A. Motor Cycles Ltd. during 1951–62. All those models (dealt with in Pitman's *The Book of the B.S.A. Twins*) had separate engines (of 497 c.c. and 646 c.c. capacity) and gearboxes.

In 1962 an entirely new range of A50 and A65 type O.H.V. vertical twins was introduced and their production has continued basically unchanged up to the present time. Some detail modifications have, of course, been made since 1962.

All 1962 and later A50 and A65 type models embody redesigned 499 c.c. and 654 c.c. four-stroke engines with unit construction of the engine and gearbox. Like the earlier A7 and A10 type models, the later models with their powerful and beautifully streamlined power units are renowned for their handsome appearance and good finish, excellent road-holding qualities, economical and silky running, genuine reliability and, above all, for their sparkling performance throughout their speed range.

As regards maintenance (the primary subject of this handbook), the designers of B.S.A. A50, A65 type models have done their utmost to reduce *essential* maintenance to the minimum. But to keep your mount in A1 condition, reduce depreciation, and to obtain and maintain maximum m.p.g., m.p.h., r.p.m., b.h.p. and pleasure at *minimum expense* you are advised carefully to observe and implement the maintenance instructions given in this handbook.

Space at the author's disposal prohibits him from delving into major overhaul and repair work. Those having sufficient mechanical skill and available facilities can, of course, tackle some of this precision work, but before doing so should consult the appropriate section in the comprehensive and well-illustrated *B.S.A. Workshop Manual* for 500 and 650 unit-construction twins.

In conclusion, the author sincerely thanks B.S.A. Motor Cycles Ltd. of Armoury Road, Birmingham, 11 (Phone: 021-772-2381), and also Amal Ltd. and Joseph Lucas Ltd., both of Birmingham, for kindly assisting him with regard to technical data and for permitting him to reproduce various excellent copyright illustrations. All except Figs. 3, 10–13, 17, 33–4, 48, 64, 76 and 78 are by courtesy of B.S.A. Motor Cycles Ltd.

A. G. LUPTON

Contents

1	Handling your B.S.A. Twin	1
2	Obtaining Good Carburation	24
3	Correct Lubrication	39
4	Lucas A.C./D.C. Lighting and Ignition	59
5	General Maintenance	64
	Index	124

1 Handling your B.S.A. Twin

You probably have already had some practical riding experience on a lightweight motor-cycle of 350 c.c. or 250 c.c. engine capacity. Whatever previous experience you may have had, you will very quickly get used to the proper and safe handling of a new or second-hand B.S.A. 500 or 650 c.c. O.H.V. vertical twin B.S.A. All A50 and A65 heavyweight type models are designed throughout for easy handling and control by experienced and inexperienced riders. Skill and confidence in riding them are quickly acquired and one soon masters their high power output and rapid acceleration.

Riding and Control Positions. On new B.S.A. A50 and A65 type mounts the riding and control positions are carefully adjusted to suit a man of *average* height and physique. With the riding position correct, the arms should be almost straight and the angle between each thigh and leg slightly less than a right-angle. Obviously riders differ considerably in height and general physique. It is therefore important on taking possession of a new or second-hand A50 or A65 type model to make sure that the handlebars and footrests are adjusted to give *you* the most comfortable and natural riding position; also to see that the hand- and foot-operated controls can be nicely operated without having to move the hands or foot from the handlebar grips or footrests respectively. The position of the comfortable dualseat is not adjustable, and the telescopic front forks have no adjustment. To suit marked variations in loading conditions the rear suspension units, however, have three adjustments for spring pressure (*see* page 120).

If the riding position of your mount is unsatisfactory, make a *combined* adjustment of: (*a*) the angle of the handlebars, (*b*) the position of the footrests, (*c*) the angle of the foot gear-change pedal, and (*d*) the angle of the various control levers on the handlebars. The necessary adjustments can be made as follows—

(*a*) To adjust the handlebars for optimum angle, loosen the four bolts which clamp them to the front fork yoke (*see* Fig. 3) and, while astride the dualseat, the hands on the grips, and the motor-cycle off its stand, move the handlebars up or down as required to give the best arm and body positions. Afterwards firmly retighten the four clamp bolts.

(b) To adjust the footrests, slacken the nuts securing the footrests to the tapered lugs and move the footrests to the most comfortable and convenient position. Note that the nut on the nearside footrest has a *left-hand thread*; the nut must therefore be turned *clockwise* to loosen it.

Fig 1 Powerful, very compact and streamlined externally—the A50, A65 type B.S.A. unit-construction O.H.V. Vertical-Twin power unit

The general design of this very modern and efficient power unit is, internally and externally, basically similar on all 1962–9 500, 650 c.c. B.S.A. four-stroke Big Twins. The A50 type engines have a bore and stroke of 65·5 mm × 74 mm, giving a capacity of 499 c.c. On the A65 type engines the bore and stroke are 75 mm × 74 mm, the engine capacity being 654 c.c. Both types of engines have a light-alloy cylinder head; dry sump lubrication, with a double-gear type oil pump; an Amal carburettor (two on 1965–9 A50C, A65L, A65S, and A65FS models); and a crankshaft-driven alternator for the Lucas a.c. ignition/lighting system.

Make quite sure that both footrests are adjusted for position so that their height is exactly equal, and that their securing nuts are very firmly re-tightened. An adjustable stop is provided for the rear-break pedal; reset this so that the brake pedal is located in the most convenient position beneath the left foot when resting on the footrest.

(c) To adjust the angle of the foot gear-change pedal, slacken the lever pinch-bolt (*see* Fig. 8) and then adjust the position of the lever on its splined shaft so that easy pivotal action of the foot about the off-side footrest effects smooth downward and upward gear changes. The gear-change lever should not deviate much from the horizontal position and, generally speaking, it is undesirable to alter appreciably its original position decided by B.S.A. Motor Cycles Ltd.

(*d*) To adjust the angle of the various handlebar control levers so that the levers come readily to hand with easy finger movement, slacken the clip-securing screws (*see* Fig. 3) and then move the control level assemblies to the most suitable angle on the handlebars within the limits provided.

Fig 2 Typical of the current A50, A65 B.S.A. unit-construction Vertical-Twin range—the 654 c.c. Model A65L "Lightning"

This mount with its big power reserve and capacity for rapid acceleration, plus its high maximum speed, is suitable for commuting in heavily built-up areas, long distance touring or streaking along modern motorways at a speed limited only by the rider's potential and the existing speed limit. For these reasons it has proved very popular in the U.S.A. as well as in the U.K. The 1968-9 range includes a decidedly fiery 654 c.c. Model A65T "Thunderbolt" and a somewhat less aggressive 499 c.c. Model A50 "Royal Star." The specification of all current models includes: a very sturdy cradle frame; telescopic front and rear suspension; front brake shoes giving powerful self-energizing action; coil ignition; pre-focus Lucas headlamps; and an external finish greatly enhanced by extensive polishing and chromium plating.

Check that the throttle twist-grip has adequate friction to prevent automatic closing. If necessary, increase the friction by means of the adjuster screw and lock-nut located beneath the under side of the throttle twist-grip at its inner end. On some models, notably those with two carburettors, an adjustable stop is provided at the twist-grip to avoid straining the cables when the slides are fully open. Also check that there is no slackness in the throttle and air slide actuating cables. Adjusters for both cables are provided mid-way in the cables on single-carburettor models, or at the carburettor end on twin-carburettor models. In both cases to take up cable slackness, release the lock-nut and screw out the adjuster sleeve as required (*see* Fig. 5).

Before Riding a B.S.A. Twin. The Law requires that you *must*—
1. Hold a reliable and up-to-date insurance policy covering all *third-party* risks and carry, or be able to produce on demand, a *cerificate of insurance*

Fig 3   Rider's view of a 1965 500 c.c. B.S.A. "Cyclone" or 650 c.c. "Lightning" showing general layout of handlebars, controls, instruments, etc.

Behind the ammeter on the Lucas headlamp are (left) a 120 m.p.h. Smiths speedometer and (right) an engine revolution counter which can register up to 8,000 r.p.m. On later models the rotary lighting switch was changed to lever operation and was mounted behind the ammeter and not to the left of it as shown above. The general layout is similar on all 1962–9 A50 and A65 type models except for the omission of an engine revolution counter on some models, the mounting of the speedometer in a headlamp nacelle on many pre-1965 models, and some variations in the location of the ignition and lighting switches.
("*Motor Cycle*"—London)

in respect of such policy. For obvious reasons if you own a valuable brand-new or little-used A50 or A65 type B.S.A. model, it is advisable to take out a fully comprehensive insurance policy.

2. Obtain and keep in a safe place the motor-cycle's registration book, and attach the current registration licence in a waterproof holder near the

front of the machine and visible from the near side. All B.S.A. vertical twins (solo or sidecar) are taxed at the rate of £10 per annum and the official form for original registration or change of ownership is Form VE 1/2 (VE 1/A for renewal). On Form VE 1/2 the engine and frame numbers must be stated. These are on the near side of the crankcase below the base of the cylinder block, and on the near side of the front engine lug respectively.

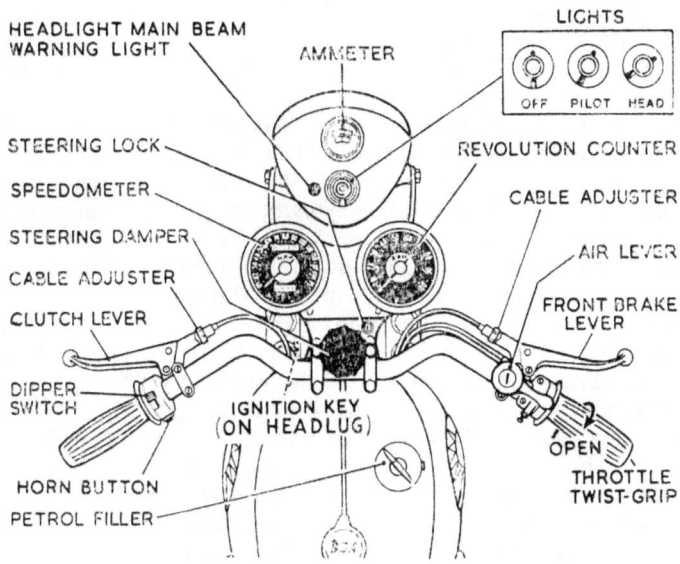

Fig 4 General layout of handlebars, controls, instruments, etc., on a 1966–8 500 c.c. B.S.A. "Cyclone" or 650 c.c. "Lightning"

This layout is identical to that shown in Fig. 3 except that the rotary or toggle (1968 models) lighting switch is mounted behind the ammeter instead of on the left of it, there is a headlamp main beam warning light, and the ignition switch (with detachable key) is mounted on the steering head lug instead of on the right of the ammeter. On some 1966–9 B.S.A. vertical twins no engine revolution counter is fitted, but the speedometer is mounted behind the headlamp as above. On later models the engine revolution counter registers up to 10,000 r.p.m. and the speedometer up to 150 m.p.h.

3. Obtain and sign a "qualified" (3 year) driver's licence (Form D.L.I.). If you are eligible for, or have, only a *provisional* (6 months) driving licence, you must pass a driving test (Form D.L. 26) before obtaining a "qualified" driver's licence. The cost of the two types of licences is £1 and the cost of a driving test is £1.75.

4. Keep the rear number plate and the speedometer in a condition such that both can be easily read by day and night. The latter must indicate within ±10 per cent accuracy when 30 m.p.h. is being exceeded.

5. If your mount is bought second-hand, check before using it that it *is* thoroughly roadworthy. The use of an unroadworthy machine is now illegal. See that the steering, lights, horn, tyres and brakes are functioning efficiently, and that neither tyre tread is excessively worn thereby giving loss of proper road grip.

6. Obtain a Ministry of Transport certificate for road worthiness from an authorized garage, dealer, or repair shop for a B.S.A. Twin used in the U.K. which was first registered more than three years ago. Subsequently this certificate must be renewed *annually*. It must be produced when applying for a registration licence in respect of renewal or change of ownership (Forms VE 1/A and VE 1/2 respectively), together with a valid *certificate of insurance* and the registration book.

The MoT certificate costs £1.25 and it is legal to ride an *untaxed* motor-cycle to a suitable testing station after making an appointment for a test. The required certificate is issued on the spot if the motor-cycle passes the statutory test for the efficiency of the tyres, brakes, steering, lamps, horn, etc.

Before taking to the road on an A50 or A65 type B.S.A., common-sense and a normal desire to "live and let live" demands that you *should*—

7. Whether an experienced or inexperienced rider, buy, read thoroughly and remember (as far as you can) the contents of the booklet, *The Highway Code*, which includes traffic signs. There are now 116 different signs! This booklet, published by H.M. Stationery Office, is profusely illustrated and obtainable from most booksellers.

8. Decide *always* to wear a smart and reliable type of safety helmet while riding short or long distances. It is not an expensive item and hospital accident statistics show that it gives great, if not complete, protection against serious head injuries in the event of its user being unfortunately involved in a major road accident. In the author's view *personal* maintenance should always be given priority to all engine and motor-cycle maintenance. Human spare parts are strictly limited!

LAYOUT AND USE OF THE CONTROLS

If you have never previously handled an A50 or A65 type B.S.A. vertical twin, before starting up and getting on the road you should become fully acquainted with the layout and use of the various controls. Most of these are mounted on the handlebars as shown in Figs. 3–6. No exhaust valve lifter is provided as on most single-cylinder four-stroke engines.

For convenience the B.S.A. control levers, switches, etc., can be divided into three main groups, namely: (1) engine controls, (2) motor-cycle controls, and (3) electrical controls for the lighting system and horn.

1. **Engine Controls, etc.** These comprise: (*a*) the throttle twist-grip, (*b*) the air lever, (*c*) the ignition switch, (*d*) the ignition cut-out button (where fitted), and (*e*) the starter pedal. Associated items are: the engine

revolution counter (where fitted), the two petrol taps, and the carburettor float-chamber tickler.

(a) *The Throttle Twist-grip.* This much used control for engine power and speed is located as shown in Fig. 5. The throttle opening is progressively increased by *anti-clockwise* turning of the grip. Adjustment for twist-grip friction and cable slackness is provided (*see* page 3). Slow-running adjustment is referred to in detail on pages 25 and 28.

(b) *The Air-control Lever.* As shown in Fig. 5, this is mounted adjacent to the throttle twist-grip and is opened by moving the lever *clockwise*

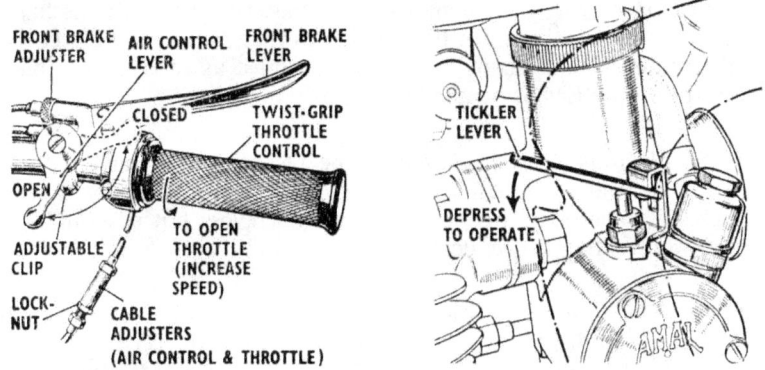

Figs 5, 6 Sketches showing (left) details of controls and cable adjusters on the off side of the handlebars, and (right) the lever control provided for the carburettor tickler on most pre-1965 500, 650 c.c. models

towards the rider. It operates a slide in each carburettor mixing chamber and controls the petrol/air ratio of the mixture. The air lever should always be kept fully open except when starting a *cold* engine. It should then be fully closed, so as to provide a rich mixture.

(c) *The Ignition Switch.* The primary purpose of this switch (operated by a detachable key) is to enable an engine with no exhaust-valve lifter to be stopped. A secondary purpose is to prevent battery discharge through the contact-breaker when the motor-cycle is parked with the engine stationary. Always remove the ignition key when leaving your mount parked in your absence for an appreciable time.

On earlier A50, A65 type models the ignition switch is mounted on the off side of the headlamp as shown in Fig. 3, or on the near side of the headlamp nacelle as shown in Fig. 7. On most 1966-9 models, however, the ignition switch is located on the near side of the steering head lug as shown in Fig. 4, the lighting switch alone being mounted on the headlamp. On 1966-9 models with the ignition switch located on the near side of the headlug, as shown in Fig. 4, the detachable ignition switch key has only two positions, namely "OFF" and "ON," obtained by turning the key fully anti-clockwise or clockwise respectively.

On many pre-1966 models with the ignition switch on the headlamp or nacelle the ignition switch key has three positions, namely "EMG," "OFF" and "ON." With the key in the *central* position the ignition is switched off. By turning the ignition key fully *clockwise* the ignition is switched on. Depressing and then turning the ignition key fully *anti-clockwise* the switch is in the "EMG" position. This position should be used only for starting the engine when the battery is so badly discharged that current for starting must be supplied to the ignition coil direct from the alternator. After starting up, the switch must as soon as possible be moved from the "EMG" to the "ON" position.

(d) *The Ignition Cut-out Button.* Some recent models have a direct-ignition system and on these models a cut-out button is mounted on the handlebars. Depressing this button stops the engine, but it should *never* be used while riding for reducing speed.

(e) *The Foot Starter.* This is of orthodox design and is located on the outside of the timing cover as shown in Fig. 8. On all recent models the pedal itself is hinged so that it can be turned away inwards after starting up the engine.

The Engine Revolution Counter. On many super-sports models an instrument recording up to 10,000 r.p.m. (on recent models) is mounted alongside the Smith's speedometer as shown in Figs. 3 and 4. It is driven from the off side of the crankshaft and its purpose is to facilitate gear changing and also warn the rider when maximum safe peak engine revolutions have been reached. Except on the 1966 A50 "Wasp" and A65 "Hornet" models the peak safe r.p.m. is 7,000, increased to 7,500 r.p.m. for 1969 650 c.c. engines. On the two above-mentioned 1966 models it is 8,250 and 7,250 r.p.m. respectively.

The Petrol Taps. Two taps are provided under the rear end of the tank, one on each side. Both taps control the main fuel supply to the carburettor. By using one tap only, a reserve fuel supply is left in the tank and this can be fed to the carburettor(s) only after turning on the second tap. To turn on either tap, pull out the knurled button and then lock it in position by turning it *anti-clockwise.*

HANDLING YOUR B.S.A. TWIN

The Carburettor Tickler. The Amal Monobloc or Concentric carburettor(s) have a spring-loaded plunger or tickler on top of the float chamber to facilitate starting a *cold* engine. On many pre-1965 A50 and A65 type models the tickler has a hand-operated lever (*see* Fig. 6) protruding from the front of the near-side panel.

Depressing the tickler prevents the float from rising in the float chamber when the petrol is turned on and therefore rapidly increases the flow of petrol into the chamber. As long as the tickler is depressed the level of petrol is not limited. For this reason use the tickler for a brief moment only, otherwise flooding of the carburettor is likely to occur. This causes an over-rich mixture which impedes starting and can in extreme cases cause damage to the engine.

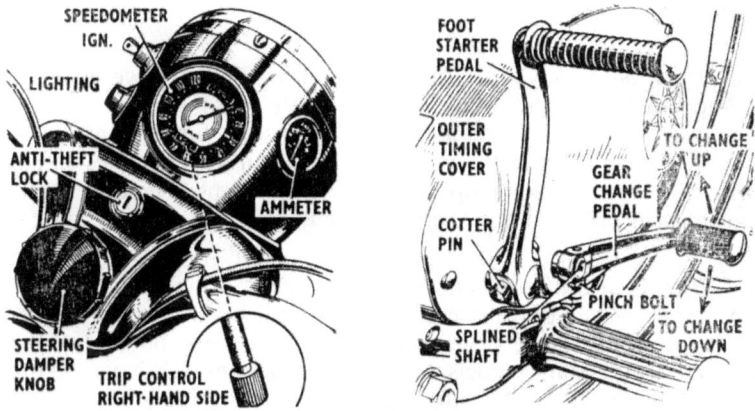

Figs 7, 8 Showing (left) location of speedometer, ammeter, rotary lighting switch, ignition switch and anti-theft lock on pre-1965 500, 650 c.c. Models with a headlamp nacelle, and (right) details of starter and gear-change pedals

2. **The Motor-cycle Controls, etc.** These comprise: (*a*) the gear-change pedal, (*b*) the clutch lever, (*c*) the front-brake lever, (*d*) the rear-brake pedal, and (*e*) the steering damper. Associated items in this case are the steering lock and the speedometer.

(*a*) *The Gear-change Pedal.* The foot-operated gear-change mechanism is of the positive-stop type designed to provide four nice, easy, quiet gear changes. Its pedal always returns to the *same* nearly horizontal position after each gear change is made and foot pressure is released.

All *downward* changes are made by *depressing* the gear-change pedal *fully* with the ball of the foot, and all *upward* changes by *raising* the pedal fully. Neutral lies between first and second gears. Note that excessive pressure must *never* be imposed on the gear-change pedal, otherwise the gear-change mechanism may become damaged. As has been mentioned on page 2, the pedal lever can, if desired, be repositioned on its shaft.

(*b*) *The Clutch Lever.* This lever, always used in conjunction with the gear-change pedal, is clipped to the near side of the handlebars as shown in Figs. 3, 4, and has finger adjustment for cable stretch.

When disconnecting engine power from the rear wheel prior to engaging a gear, *complete* disengagement of the clutch plates must always be made by squeezing the lever *fully*. When reconnecting engine power after making a gear change, the clutch-lever must be released slowly and progressively. Fierce and sudden engagement of the clutch-plates is bad for the transmission and engine.

(*c*) *The Front-brake Lever.* The front and rear brakes have shoes of the cam-operated type and when braking, both brakes should be applied *simultaneously* and not separately. The hand lever for the front brake is pivoted, as may be seen in Figs. 4, 5, near the air lever and has a knurled finger-adjuster for taking up cable stretch. On most models a second adjustment is provided at the brake-plate (*see* Fig. 67).

(*d*) *The Rear-brake Pedal.* A knurled self-locking hand adjuster is provided at the end of the sleeve or rod used for brake cable or rod operation respectively. Cable operation is provided on the off side of earlier 1962 A50, A65 "Star" models, but all subsequent models have rod operation. A *single* rod is used on the *near side*, except on the 1962–5 A50, A65 "Star" models and the 1964–5 A65R "Rocket." On these models *two* linked rods are provided on the *off side* of the machine. They are actuated from the rear-brake pedal via a transverse cross-shaft to the near-side end of which the pedal is fitted.

The rear-brake pedal is mounted on the splined end of the cross-shaft as shown in Fig. 9. An arm formed on the pedal lever contacts an adjustable stop-screw which should always be set so that the brake pedal itself lies comfortably below the ball of the left foot, ready for immediate operation. Note that an adjustment of the pedal position usually necessitates readjustment of the hand adjuster on the end of the sleeve or rod in the case of a cable- or rod-operated brake respectively. Detailed instructions on brake and other motor-cycle adjustments are given in Chapter 5.

(*e*) *The Steering Damper.* Tightening down the steering damper knob (*see* Fig. 7) increases the friction damping and front-fork stability, but the steering characteristics of all B.S.A. vertical twins are so good that when riding a 500 or 650 c.c. model solo it is unnecessary and undesirable to tighten down the damper at all except when riding over rough road surfaces or at high speed. Riding solo at low speed with the damper tightened down can adversely affect steering. On a sidecar outfit, however, it is advisable *always* to keep the steering damper tightened down slightly and to increase its tightening to suit road and speed conditions.

The Steering Lock. Switching off the ignition and removing the detachable ignition key does not prevent the theft of a motor-cycle by someone wheeling it away. An anti-theft lock is therefore built into the top fork

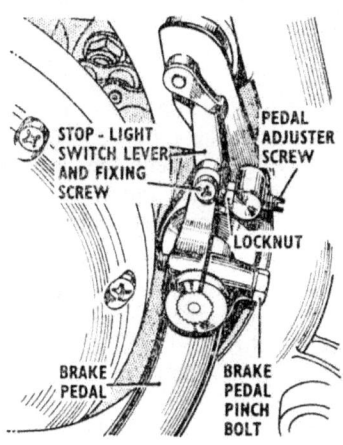

Fig 9 Showing adjustment for rear-brake pedal position and automatic stop-light switch

The arrangement shown applies to 1962-4 models with cable or rod brake operation. On later machines the same general principle is used.

yoke. A Yale key is provided to operate this steering lock. Note that it is detrimental to insert oil into the keyhole positioned as shown in Figs. 4, 7.

To operate the built-in steering lock, turn the handlebars to the *left* and then turn the key in the lock to release the plunger which registers with a special frame lug. Afterwards remove the key, which should be attached to a key-ring or kept in a wallet to prevent accidental loss and serious trouble on the road.

The Central Stand. All 1962-9 B.S.A. vertical twins have a spring-loaded roll-up type central stand which requires little effort to operate. The knack of pulling the motor-cycle backwards and slightly upwards by means of the combined hand rail and dualseat support is very soon mastered. To remove the machine from its central stand it is only necessary to push the motor-cycle gently forward, when the stand automatically springs up clear of the ground.

Using a Prop Stand. If you have fitted a B.S.A. or a proprietary make of prop stand to your mount, avoid using it on soft ground such as a tarred road surface in hot weather. Also when positioning the machine on a prop stand, be sure first to turn off the petrol, otherwise some flooding of the carburettor is likely to occur.

The Speedometer. A Smiths trip-type 120 m.p.h. speedometer is mounted on the headlamp nacelle on pre-1965 models, or on later models behind the headlamp adjacent to the engine revolution counter (where fitted) as shown in Figs. 3, 4. A white line on most instruments emphasizes the 30 m.p.h. calibration, the usual speed limit in the U.K. for "built-up" areas.

The "trip" mileage recorder can be reset to zero by rotating *clockwise* the flexible trip-control located at the rear of or on the right-hand side of the speedometer according to the type of B.S.A. model concerned. On some earlier machines having a nacelle the flexible trip-control (located below the nacelle) is spring-loaded and it is necessary to pull the trip control out, before resetting the mileage recorder.

3. The Electrical Controls, etc. Disregarding the controls solely concerned with engine running (i.e. the ignition switch and cut-out button), the remaining controls are: (*a*) the lighting switch, (*b*) the dipper switch, (*c*) the stop-light switch, and (*d*) the horn button.

(*a*) *The Lighting Switch.* This rotary or lever-operated (1968-9) switch, with finger-operated grip, or toggle, is positioned on the Lucas headlamp to the left of or behind the ammeter as shown in Figs. 3, 4, or on pre-1965 models on the headlamp nacelle as shown in Fig. 7. The three rotary type switch positions are indicated at the top right-hand corner of Fig. 4 and are as follows—

(1) With the switch finger-grip in the vertical ("OFF") position *all* lights are extinguished.

(2) With the finger grip turned *clockwise* to the second ("PILOT") position the headlamp pilot bulb, the tail-lamp, instrument lights, and sidecar lamps (where fitted) are switched on.

(3) With the finger grip turned *clockwise* to the third ("HEAD") position the headlamp pre-focus main bulb, the tail-lamp, instrument lights and sidecar lamps (where fitted) are switched on.

On all 1968-9 B.S.A. vertical twins, which have a Lucas three-position lever-operated type 57SA lighting switch located behind the ammeter, the above-mentioned lighting effects are obtained with the toggle-type lever moved *from left to right* to positions 1, 2, 3 respectively. This redesigned switch has no actual markings to indicate the lever position.

Note that in all three of the above switch positions the alternator charging rate varies according to the state of charge of the battery mounted

HANDLING YOUR B.S.A. TWIN   13

as shown in Fig. 31 on the near side of the motor-cycle. As the battery becomes almost fully charged the alternator charging rate decreases and vice versa.

(b) *The Headlamp Dipper Switch.* As shown in Figs. 3, 4, this switch is mounted in an annular housing (adjustable for position after loosening the locking-screw) adjacent to the near-side handlebar grip. It controls the double-filament main bulb in the Lucas headlamp and enables the rider to switch from the main beam to the dipped beam as required.

(c) *The Stop-light Switch.* This switch is automatically operated by the movement of the rear-brake pedal and controls the filament of the stop-tail lamp bulb so as to indicate braking. An extension from the rear-brake pedal (*see* Fig. 9) operates the stop-light switch.

Note that when an adjustment for rear-brake pedal position (*see* page 114) has to be made, it is necessary afterwards to check that the stop-light still functions when the brake pedal is depressed, and that the light goes out when the pedal is released. The extension can if necessary be slightly repositioned by loosening its screw with the special screwdriver provided in the tool kit.

(d) *The Horn Button.* The horn-operating button is mounted in the same annular housing as the headlamp dipper switch and both these controls function with the lighting switch in any of its three positions. On B.S.A. models not provided with battery lighting the horn button is independently mounted on the left side of the handlebars and can be operated only when the engine is running.

The Ammeter. This electrical instrument is mounted on the Lucas headlamp or on the headlamp nacelle (*see* Figs. 3, 4, 7). It indicates at a glance whether the alternator is charging the battery or whether the latter is being discharged. The charging rates are shown on the ammeter dial as "Charge" (+) or "Discharge" (−). The alternator charge is automatically controlled and varies, but, unless the battery is charged to maximum capacity, at least a small charge should be indicated by the ammeter needle when the engine is running with all lamps switched off.

ENGINE STARTING, ETC.

Petrol and Oil Replenishment. On a brand new machine or one purchased second-hand from a dealer, or privately, make sure that the petrol and oil tanks, the gearbox, and the oil-bath primary chaincase are adequately topped-up with petrol and oil. Also check that the battery cells are topped-up with electrolyte to the correct level and fully charged. These preliminaries are normally dealt with as a routine matter by the dealer from whom a B.S.A.

twin is bought, but such is not always the case where a machine is bought second-hand from a previous owner.

The petrol tank capacity varies on different models from 2 to 4 gallons (5 gallons on some 1967–8 "Spitfire" models). Petrol tank filler-caps are of the quick-release type except on 1968–9 models where snap-action caps are provided. Always run on a good premium grade of petrol, especially if your mount is a super-sports type with a high compression ratio. If your engine has a C.R. of 10·5 to 1, it is essential to replenish with 100 octane fuel. Where a fibre-glass tank is fitted, *never* replenish with a fuel containing alcohol. During the running-in period for a new or reconditioned engine it is beneficial, but not essential, to add a shot of upper-cylinder lubricant such as Redex to every gallon of petrol poured into the tank.

The oil tank filler-cap is readily accessible and replenishment does not necessitate the removal of the detachable panel from the off-side of the motor-cycle. Tank capacity is 5 pints (5½ pints on pre-1966 models).

Always replenish the oil tank with one of the brands and grades of engine oils recommended by B.S.A. Motor Cycles Ltd. (*see* page 42). The normal oil level required for maximum efficiency is *up to the lowest edge of the filler-cap neck*. On 1966–9 models a dip-stick indicating the maximum and minimum safe oil levels is attached to the filler-cap. On 1962 A50 and A65 models there is an appropriate marking on the outside of the oil tank.

Replenishment of the B.S.A. gearbox (in unit construction with the engine) should be effected with one of the six oils recommended on page 50. Gearbox lubrication is dealt with in detail on that page. On all 1962–9 A50, A65 type models the capacity of the four-speed gearbox is ⅞ pint. and the oil level is predetermined by a stand-pipe built-in with the oil drain plug. This plug must always be left in position during actual replenishment. For 1968–9 models the stand-pipe was replaced by a dip-stick attached to the gearbox filler-cap.

The capacity of the oil-bath chaincase is ¼ pint and the chaincase should be replenished with suitable oil as described on page 52 through the filler-cap orifice on the case *to the level of the drain-plug screw orifice*.

Setting Controls for Starting (Cold Engine). With the engine quite cold, the following is the correct control setting normally required to effect a quick start—

1. Open fully *one* petrol tap, keeping the other tap closed to ensure the maintenance of a reserve petrol supply in the tank. To avoid any possible confusion, it is best when starting-up and riding always to keep the *near-side* petrol-tap closed.

2. Make absolutely sure that *neutral* (positioned between first and second gears) has been selected. An indicator is *not* provided on any 1962–9 A50 and A65 type B.S.A. models. If the machine is on its central stand it should be possible to spin the rear wheel freely by hand; if it is *not* on its

HANDLING YOUR B.S.A. TWIN   15

central stand it should be possible to move the machine backwards and forwards without encountering resistance caused by engine compression. Another obvious test is to exert pressure on the kick-starter pedal and note

Fig 10   Off-side view of 1967 654 c.c. Model A65L B.S.A. "Lightning"

The 1968–9 version is almost identical except for the provision of twin Amal Concentric type carburettors instead of the two Monobloc type instruments illustrated, and the fitting inside the timing case of a new design of Lucas contact-breaker assembly having independent adjustment of the contact gap and contact positions. The latter internal modification has been included to enable the ignition timing to be set more accurately.

Key to Fig. 10

1. Oil tank filler-cap with (1966–8) dip-stick attached
2. One of two snap fasteners for removing panel to give access to oil tank, pipes and filter
3. One of two Vokes dry-felt type air cleaners clipped to the carburettor air intakes
4. Throttle-stop adjusting screw
5. Pilot-air adjusting screw
6. Off-side petrol tap
7. Light-alloy cylinder head
8. Circular cover for contact-breaker and automatic advance-and-retard mechanism
9. The ignition coil assembly
10. Kick-starter pedal (hinged) cottered to its shaft
11. The off-side footrest (both are adjustable for position)
12. Gearbox filter cap
13. Foot gearchange pedal (adjustable for position on its splined shaft)
14. Driving cable connection for engine revolution counter
15. Lucas electric horn

whether this causes the motor-cycle to move forward; if the machine does move forward, obviously a gear is engaged.

If you suspect a gear to be engaged, stand astride your mount and *depress* the foot gear-change pedal *fully* twice or three times in succession while simultaneously easing the motor-cycle backwards and forwards to enable the gears in the gearbox to rotate as required. When you have definitely engaged bottom (first) gear *raise* the gear-change pedal through *half* its normal stroke in order to select *neutral*.

3. Close the air-control lever (*anti-clockwise*) completely and open the throttle(s) very slightly by turning the twist-grip a small amount (not more than about ⅛ in. as measured at the rim of the twist-grip).

4. Flood the carburettor(s) very slightly by depressing *momentarily* the float-chamber tickler(s).

5. Switch on the ignition (all coil-ignition models) by turning the key in the ignition switch fully *clockwise*. The timing of the ignition is *automatically* fully retarded for starting, and progressively advanced as the engine speed increases.

Setting Controls for Starting (Warm Engine). If the engine of your mount is already thoroughly warmed up, the correct control setting is as previously described for a *cold* engine, but do not flood the carburettor(s) and move the air-control lever *clockwise* from its fully closed position so that it is *fully open*.

If the engine is not warmed up to normal running temperature but has slightly cooled down during a temporary halt, it is usually advisable to set the air-control lever so that it is about *half-way* between the fully open and fully closed positions. However, different engines can be temperamentally different and it is wisest where a partially warmed-up engine is concerned to experiment until the best setting of the air-control lever for quick starting is obtained.

Emergency Starting Procedure. If you own a pre-1966 model and its battery has suddenly become badly discharged, you can start up without making use of the battery for coil ignition by following the control settings previously given, with the exception of instruction No. 5. In this case depress the ignition key in the ignition switch and turn it fully *anti-clockwise* to the "EMG" position, keeping it in this position until the engine is started. It must then be turned fully *clockwise* to the "ON" position.

Beware of Flooding Down-draught Carburettors Excessively. All B.S.A. A50 and A65 type vertical twins have down-draught Amal Monobloc or Concentric type carburettors fitted. Because these instruments are inclined downwards at an angle to the cylinder head it is therefore important *never* to flood them excessively before starting up the engine.

Excessive flooding can result in *neat* petrol entering the combustion

… chambers via the induction manifold and thereby breaking down the vital oil film between the piston rings and cylinder bores and, in extreme cases, causing serious wear through friction. In the case of a new or reconditioned engine which has not been run-in, the risk is very considerable.

Use of Starter Pedal. After carefully setting the engine controls as previously described, push down the starter pedal, preferably while standing astride the dualseat, until the compression of the mixture in one of the cylinders causes resistance. Then without releasing the pressure, deliver with the right foot a deliberate and vigorous downward thrust on the starter pedal. The engine should fire.

If it fails to fire at the first attempt, repeat the above procedure as required, but avoid rapid kicks; this does not facilitate starting and is liable to damage the internal kick-starter mechanism. Where the engine is in sound mechanical condition and the carburettor adjustment is correct, it will probably fire at the first or second attempt. Immediately the engine fires, open the air-control lever *fully*.

Warming Up a Cold Engine. This should be done at a *moderate speed* for some minutes. Warming up the engine too slowly, though sounding good, does in fact prevent the oil pump functioning fast enough to ensure thorough oil circulation throughout the power unit, thereby incurring some risk of excessive wear and/or damage; it also can cause incomplete combustion of atomized fuel in cold combustion chambers which in turn can cause "low temperature condensation." In simple language this means condensation in and corrosion of the cylinder bores. This phenomenon can be detrimental *and* expensive.

Warming up a cold engine too fast can generate excessive heat and friction between moving parts before the circulation of oil has become normal throughout the engine. Stop warming up your engine as soon as it attains its normal running temperature, and never allow it to tick over for too long after it has warmed up. If its tick-over speed, with the throttle twist-grip fully closed, is not such as to give moderate r.p.m., make the necessary slow-running adjustment as described in Chapter 2.

Before moving off on a run of any appreciable length, always make a habit of checking that the oil *is* circulating properly by removing the oil-tank filler-cap and observing whether oil is being ejected from the orifice of the oil return pipe.

ON THE ROAD

The Gearbox and Engine r.p.m. Always remember that the power output of your engine under load is roughly proportional to its r.p.m. (engine revolutions per minute); the primary purpose of the four-speed gearbox is to ensure those r.p.m. being maintained reasonably high under *all* conditions of road, weather, load, etc. Full and proper use of the gearbox should therefore always be made to prevent undue stresses being imposed on the engine and transmission. This is of special importance in the case of a new B.S.A. twin.

All gear changes should be made smoothly and *in good time*. Under no circumstances allow the engine to labour with an excessively *high* gear engaged having regard to the prevailing circumstances. This is a form of cruelty likely to result in a hostile reaction! It is far less cruel to cause the engine to run at slightly excessive r.p.m. in a *lower* gear, provided that the throttle opening is not excessive.

Note that when rapidly accelerating from a moderate road speed in top gear it is desirable to boost up engine r.p.m. by changing down into third gear for a brief period. When endeavouring to obtain maximum possible acceleration and speed from a B.S.A. twin (not recommended except on motorways) peak engine revolutions should be obtained, but not exceeded, during the necessary gear changes. This particularly applies to changing from third to top gear when attempting to get the maximum speed out of a sports or super-sports model. Models of this type usually have an engine revolution counter fitted and this should be observed most carefully to see that *safe* peak revolutions (*see* page 8) are not exceeded. Disastrous consequences can result from r.p.m. becoming grossly excessive! The exhaust noise does, of course, convey a rough idea of r.p.m., but should not be relied upon, especially if it develops into a snarl!

To Engage First Gear. Sitting comfortably on the dualseat and with the engine ticking-over at a moderate speed, in neutral, disengage the clutch and after a short pause *depress* the foot gear-change pedal *fully* until bottom gear is engaged and felt to engage. To facilitate full pedal movement and gear engagement with the motor-cycle stationary, it is sometimes necessary to move the machine slightly forwards and backwards while maintaining a light pressure on the gear-change pedal. This applies to most motor-cycles having gearboxes provided with foot gear-change control.

In the case of a brand new B.S.A. vertical twin, or a used model with a reconditioned clutch, some difficulty in engaging first gear is sometimes encountered for a short period because of sticking clutch-plates. The usually successful remedy is to stop the engine by means of the ignition switch or cut-out button (if fitted) and then sharply operate the kick-starter several times with the clutch fully disengaged.

Starting Off. With first (bottom) gear properly engaged, and with the engine ticking over at a moderate speed, slightly open the throttle and gently and progressively engage the clutch until the power output of the engine takes up the full load imposed on it and the motor-cycle moves off.

Be careful to avoid excessive throttle opening until the handlebar clutch-lever is fully released. As your mount gathers speed and momentum, gradually give the engine more throttle to prevent any tendency for it to stall and cause transmission snatch. It is nice to "get away from it all," but do this and make all subsequent gear changes with a nicely phased and coordinated movement of the controls and machine.

Changing Up. All upward gear changes from first to second, third and fourth gears require the same general procedure, bearing in mind the previous remarks about the appropriate synchronizing of the gearbox and engine r.p.m. and safe maximum peak r.p.m. With the B.S.A. constant-mesh four-speed gearbox, actual gear-crashing even at safe maximum engine r.p.m. is quite impossible and the technique of good changing-up is readily mastered. Each change to a higher gear should be made in the following manner.

Close the throttle twist-grip and simultaneously disconnect all engine power from the gearbox and transmission by fully disengaging the clutch; pause a split second and then *raise* the foot gear-change pedal to its *full* extent, exerting steady lift with the toe until the next higher gear is felt to engage. Afterwards remove the toe from the pedal and allow the latter to return to its normal position (nearly horizontal), ready for changing up into the next higher gear.

To compensate for the increased load imposed on the power unit, open the throttle as required, immediately and progressively, after making each upward gear change. With reasonable patience and moderate experience, smooth and quiet gear changing becomes an "automatic" procedure.

Changing Down. Changing down to a lower gear, unlike upward gear changes, always involves *increasing* the engine r.p.m. relative to those of the gearbox layshaft during each gear change.

Throttle down your engine until the machine travels at a cruising speed normal for the lower gear to be engaged. Then simultaneously disengage the clutch and slightly open the throttle. Pause a split second and then *depress* the foot gear-change pedal to its *full* extent with foot pressure until the next lower gear is felt to engage. Re-engage the clutch immediately and remove the foot from the gear-change pedal.

Note that after acquiring considerable experience in gear changing you should not find it necessary, except when hill climbing, to use the full changing-down procedure, previously described, for each individual gear change. Instead you can throttle down the engine until your mount is travelling slowly and then disengage the clutch and *depress* the gear-change lever fully three times in quick succession (with the clutch disengaged), assuming top gear is already in engagement. During each quick movement of the gear-change pedal, "blip" (throttle-up) the engine slightly. After bottom gear is felt to engage, close the throttle to its normal position, re-engage the clutch and progressively open the throttle to obtain the desired engine and road speed.

To Obtain "Neutral" from First Gear. Carefully brake the machine to a halt with the throttle twist-grip closed, disengage the clutch and then *raise* the gear-change pedal gently and *slightly* until the gear-change mechanism is felt to click into "neutral" (between first and second gears). Raising the pedal excessively will, of course, result in second gear being engaged.

Stopping a B.S.A. Twin. The normal procedure is as follows—
1. Close the throttle twist-grip completely.
2. Apply *both* brakes simultaneously and progressively.
3. Completely disengage the clutch.
4. As the motor-cycle slows to a halt, engage first gear, followed by "neutral" if it is intended to stop or park the machine for an appreciable time. Endeavour to carry out operations 2 and 3 together.

To stop the engine, switch off the ignition by means of the ignition-switch key or by depressing the cut-out button (if fitted).

Parking Your Mount. Always turn off the petrol tap in use when parking a B.S.A. twin even for a short time. This will eliminate any risk of neat petrol entering the combustion chambers in the event of flooding occurring on an Amal carburettor inclined at an appreciable angle to the cylinder head. On sports and super-sports models the angle of inclination is considerable.

On a B.S.A. twin it is important, besides turning off the petrol, to switch off the ignition when leaving a machine parked for a considerable time. If the ignition switch (*see* page 7) is left switched on and the contact-breaker contacts happen to be closed, some battery discharge is sure to result.

To minimize the risk of theft it is also advisable when parking your mount always to remove the detachable ignition key, and when parking it out of sight for a considerable period also to operate the B.S.A. steering lock (*see* page 11) by means of the key provided for this purpose. When parking your mount by the roadside at night it must be jacked up so that its *near* side is aligned with the kerb, and, unless the machine is illuminated by a street lamp, the headlamp pilot bulb and the rear lamp must be kept illuminated.

Use Both Brakes Together. Road speed should be controlled as far as possible by sensible use of the throttle-twist grip, and when brake action is necessary to reduce speed, use both of them *together* and not separately. This ensures maximum braking power and imposes minimum stresses on the motor-cycle and tyres. Never use the clutch or ignition cut-out button for reducing speed.

Climbing and Descending Hills. When climbing a steepish hill, especially if a sidecar is fitted, it is desirable to make full use of the gearbox and to make all downward gear changes *in good time*. It is essential to maintain reasonably high engine r.p.m. (*see* page 8) during a climb and never to permit the engine to labour (indicated by a tendency for knocking to occur).

When descending a steep hill, retardation is assisted by fully closing the throttle twist-grip and making use of engine compression to assist braking, assisted by changing down if necessary. Note that it is illegal to coast down a hill in "neutral."

RUNNING-IN

Be Very Careful for 1,500 *Miles*. When riding a new or reconditioned A50 or A65 type B.S.A. twin you *must* handle the machine, and run-in the engine, with the greatest care during the first 1,000–1,500 miles. You must also be meticulous about certain routine maintenance matters during the whole running-in period. These matters are briefly outlined at the end of this chapter.

By exercising patience until your speedometer trip registers about 1,250 miles you will find that your mount's performance progressively improves and trouble-free running is greatly extended. There naturally follows reduced depreciation in regard to its market value. Impatience and carelessness can *permanently* spoil performance and cause a general "devaluation." Why is careful running-in so essential?

Cylinder-bore and bearing surfaces when new *look* dead smooth, but actually they are covered with fine precision-tool marks (*see* Fig. 11) which are quite invisible to the naked eye but very defined if examined under a lens. Until these tool marks disappear and a mirror-like gloss and uniform hardness spreads over all moving surfaces in contact with each other, excessive local friction and heat generation is very apt to occur, followed by the vital oil film between moving surfaces breaking down at one or more places with disastrous and often expensive consequences. This is especially applicable to the two cylinder bores and their associated pistons and rings.

Points to Watch. Piston temperature must never be allowed to become excessive during running-in, and for this reason excessive speed and/or big throttle openings must at all costs be avoided. During the initial stages of running-in, one-third to one-half throttle should not be exceeded in *any* gear, and in the case of a brand new B.S.A. model the speed limitations stated on its running-in label should be strictly adhered to during the first 500 miles.

After covering about 500 miles the throttle openings can be *progressively* stepped up, but throughout the whole of the running-in period it is most important to avoid violent acceleration and/or allowing the engine to labour by climbing hills with an excessively high gear engaged. Smooth throttle control and the selection of gears appropriate to the prevailing conditions are the two factors which merit special attention. During running-in always endeavour to keep the engine running as "light" as possible and never handle the machine in a manner likely to cause overheating. After running-in is completed it is advisable to "balance" the two wheels and it is, of course, then permissible to run your mount on full throttle.

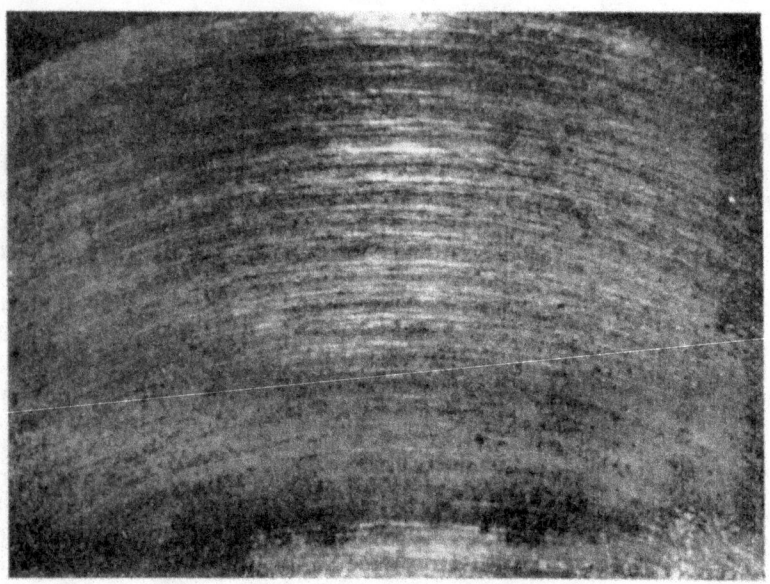

Fig 11   Observed under a powerful lens, the cylinder-bore surfaces (when new) are covered with numerous circular tool marks

Only by careful and progressive running-in of a new or reconditioned engine can tool marks of the type shown be eliminated and rough metal surfaces be restored to smoothness, with a mirror-like gloss. A smooth surface is necessary to ensure maximum lubrication and minimum friction and heat.

But even on modern motorways the use of full throttle for prolonged periods is not recommended. The engine and the Minister of Transport prefer a reasonable cruising speed. This will prolong the life of your engine and possibly yours also!

Maintenance During Running-in. The following deserves close attention—
1. Keep the oil tank and gearbox well topped-up (*see* pages 13 and 50).
2. After completing 250 miles drain and replenish the oil tank with

HANDLING YOUR B.S.A. TWIN

fresh oil of the correct brand and grade; also clean the tank and crankcase filters (*see* pages 42 and 44). Repeat after covering 500 miles.

3. Drain and refill the gearbox with fresh oil of the recommended brand and grade after running for 500 miles (*see* page 51).

4. Should symptoms of piston seizure result from running at excessive speed and/or with excessive throttle opening, *instantly* close the throttle and fully disengage the clutch. This forthright action often prevents anything but slight smearing on the piston lands between the rings; a skilful mechanic will quickly remove all such detrimental effects.

5. Remove and clean, or get cleaned, both sparking plugs (*see* page 67) after riding about 1,000 miles. Dirty plugs will give dirty riding!

6. During running-in some initial bedding-down of various components occurs and it is advisable to check rather more frequently than usual the valve clearances, the contact-breaker gaps, the clutch adjustment, all control settings, etc. Also do not omit to check periodically *all* external bolts and nuts for tightness. Some slackenening off is normal and is to be expected. Do not wait for a squeak or rattle to develop. In conclusion, treat and handle your mount in such a manner that *you* do not become the target for a wailing ambulance.

2 Obtaining Good Carburation

Good carburation is essential to good engine performance. After making exhaustive road and bench tests, B.S.A. Motor Cycles Ltd. have obtained and included for all their 1962–9 A50 and A65 type twins the optimum carburettor settings for normal road use; these settings aim at giving the best general performance combined with low fuel consumption. For obvious reasons it is presumptuous to attempt to improve on the maker's recommended settings (tabulated on page 31). Where climatic conditions are greatly different from those in the U.K. this does not necessarily apply.

Although jet sizes, throttle valve cut-away, and the jet-needle position should not normally be changed, it is sometimes necessary to alter the slow-running adjustment, with the throttle twist-grip fully closed, in order to obtain a nice engine tick-over, and it is desirable about every 5,000 miles to remove any foreign impurities which may have accumulated in the carburettor float-chamber. After a considerable mileage has been covered it is wise to remove, dismantle, inspect and thoroughly clean the whole carburettor.

Two Types of Amal Carburettors Fitted. The instruments fitted as standard to 1962–9 B.S.A. twins comprise two distinct types: the "Monobloc" and the "Concentric" (the latter officially known as Series 6C0 and 900). The former type has been fitted to all 1962–7 A50 and A65 models except the 1966 and 1967 Model A65S "Spitfires" which have the special GP2 and the latest "Concentric" respectively. A "Concentric" type carburettor is also fitted to *all* 1968–9 twins.

Note that some B.S.A. twins (e.g. "Royal Star" and "Thunderbolt") have a single carburettor fitted but others, mostly of the super-sports type (e.g. 1966 "Wasp," "Cyclone," "Hornet," "Lightning" and "Spitfire" models) have twin carburettors of the same type fitted to the cylinder head. Most 1962 and later models are provided with a "pill-box" type air filter.

Technical Details. The Amal carburettor controls are briefly referred to on page 7 and comprise the throttle twist-grip and the air lever, the latter normally being closed only for starting a *cold* engine. In all other respects the action of the "Monobloc" and "Concentric" type carburettors

OBTAINING GOOD CARBURATION

is entirely automatic and not subject to control by the rider. In both cases their functioning is basically similar, supplying a mixture of petrol vapour and air to the combustion chambers of the engine, mixed in the correct proportions.

Owing to strict limitations of space available to the author, he is unable to describe in detail the precise functioning of the two types of Amal carburettors fitted to B.S.A. twins. Full functioning details are, however, included in Amal Lists Nos. 102/3 and 117/3 (obtainable from Amal Ltd. of Holdford Road, Witton, Birmingham, 6) dealing with "Monobloc" and "Concentric" type carburettors respectively. The two sectional views shown in Figs. 12 and 13 illustrate some important details of the two types of carburettors, and the exploded views of the complete carburettors (see Figs. 15 and 16) provide a good idea of their general design and layout.

Is the Slow-running Mixture Correct? Possibly it is; possibly it is not! An *excessively rich* slow-running mixture results in a tendency for the engine to run on the pilot jet under normal riding conditions. An *excessively weak* slow-running mixture causes the engine to run hot and irregularly and to "spit-back" in the lower speed range. Obviously it is important to obtain a slow-running mixture which combines petrol vapour and air in the right proportions.

If the slow-running adjustment and carburettor setting are correct, and the carburettor and engine are both in sound mechanical condition, sharply opening the throttle should produce no black smoke from the exhaust pipes. With the mixture correct, the exhaust flames (observed at open exhaust ports) should be of a *whitish-blue* colour. Listen to the exhaust note; it should be clear and crisp. In the lower speed range general performance of the engine should be good, and without any "woolliness" or "flat spots" occurring. There should also be no tendency for the engine to "spit back" when riding slowly or allowing the engine to tick over with neutral engaged.

If the carburettor is *excessively rich* general performance and idling become erratic, and sharply opening the throttle often causes some black smoke to emerge from the exhaust pipes. The colour of the exhaust flame from an open exhaust port is *yellow* in the event of the mixture being excessively rich. Such a mixture does, of course, cause the petrol consumption to rise steeply.

ADJUSTMENTS AND FAULTS

Slow-running Adjustment (Single Carburettor). To correct poor slow-running due to an incorrect mixture, a combined adjustment of the pilot-air adjusting screw and the throttle stop must be made. The adjustment procedure is the same on all single-carburettor models (e.g. "Royal Star" and "Thunderbolt") whether an Amal "Monobloc" or a "Concentric"

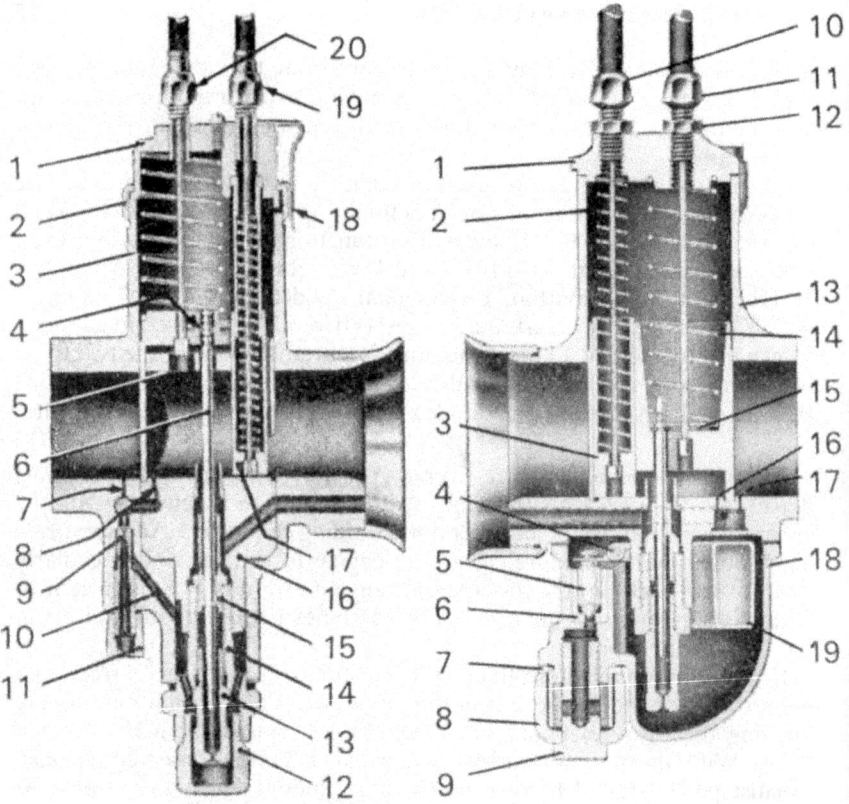

Figs 12, 13 Showing (left) sectional view through mixing chamber, jet block, etc., of Amal "Monobloc" carburettor, and (right) similar view of Amal "Concentric" instrument showing concentric float-chamber details

Key to Fig 12 ("Monobloc")
1. Mixing chamber top
2. Mixing-chamber cap ring
3. Carburettor body
4. Jet-needle clip
5. Throttle valve
6. Jet needle
7. Pilot outlet
8. Pilot by-pass
9. Pilot jet
10. Petrol feed to 9
11. Cover nut for 9
12. Main jet cover-nu
13. Main jet
14. Holder for 13
15. Needle jet
16. Jet block
17. Air valve
18. Spring for 2
19. Cable adjuster (air)
20. Cable adjuster (throttle)

Key to Fig 13 ("Concentric")
1. Mixing chamber top
2. Spring for air valve
3. Air vlave
4. Float spindle
5. Float needle
6. Seating for 5
7. Gauze filter
8. Banjo
9. Securing bolt for 8
10. Cable adjuster (air)
11. Cable adjuster (throttle)
12. Locknut for 11
13. Carburettor body
14. Spring for throttle valve
15. Jet-needle clip
16. Pilot by-pass
17. Pilot outlet
18. Float chamber
19. Float

OBTAINING GOOD CARBURATION

type carburettor is fitted. Always make the adjustment required with the engine thoroughly *warmed up*.

With the throttle twist-grip fully closed, the air-control lever opened fully, *screw inwards* the pilot-air adjusting screws (*see* Fig. 14) until the petrol/air mixture is excessively rich and the engine begins to run irregularly. Then make the engine run evenly by *screwing outwards* the pilot-air adjusting screw. When weakening the mixture in this manner, be careful not to over-weaken the mixture, otherwise it may spit back through the

Fig 14 Showing throttle-stop and pilot-air adjusting screws, etc., on one of two Amal "Monobloc" carburettors fitted to a 654 c.c. B.S.A. Twin

The slow-running adjustment for B.S.A. twins fitted with Amal "Concentric" carburettor(s) is the same as for machines with "Monobloc" carburettor(s), but small "O" rings replace coil springs to secure adjusting screws on the later "Concentric" instruments.

1. Vokes air cleaner
2. Amal "Monobloc" carburettor
3. Throttle-stop
4. Locking screw for jet block
5. Pilot-air adjusting screw
6. Off-side petrol tap

carburettor and possibly cause the engine to stop on opening the throttle twist-grip.

When you have made the above adjustment and the engine ticks over evenly you may find that its r.p.m. are excessively high. The remedy for this trouble is to *unscrew* the throttle-stop screw (*see* Fig. 14) until the engine runs regularly and evenly at a moderately fast tick-over speed. Should you find it necessary to make a considerable adjustment of the throttle-stop screw, you will probably find that a further adjustment of the pilot-air adjusting screw will be necessary in order to effect a correctly proportioned slow-running mixture. For the reasons previously mentioned, avoid a combined adjustment resulting in an excessively slow tick-over speed. Generally speaking, it is wise to aim at a moderately fast tick-over with the mixture just *approaching* the weak side.

The final test of a slow-running adjustment is to rev the engine up and down sharply several times with the machine stationary and while riding. The exhaust note should be nice and crisp and there should be no "flat spots" or "spitting back" when the throttle twist-grip is quickly turned. Acceleration should also be crisp and smooth.

Slow-running Adjustment (Twin Carburettors). Where two "Monobloc" or "Concentric" type Amal carburettors are fitted (i.e. on *all* 1962–9 B.S.A. models except the "Royal Star" and "Thunderbolt") the above procedure is applicable in respect of each individual carburettor, but the following three points should be carefully observed—

1. Should your engine fail to respond quickly and develop a "flat spot" when opening the throttle from a tick-over position, consider the possibility of wear of one or both of the throttle valves and/or needle jets. If close inspection reveals serious wear, renew the part(s) as required before attempting a slow-running adjustment.

2. Make an individual adjustment of the L.H. and R.H. carburettors for slow-running. Detach the h.t. lead from the off-side sparking plug and run the power unit with the throttle twist-grip closed, using the near-side cylinder only. Then make a combined adjustment of the pilot-air adjusting screw and the throttle-stop screw on the L.H. carburettor.

Switch off the ignition, remove the h.t. lead from the near-side sparking plug, and reconnect the h.t. lead to the off-side sparking plug. Start up the engine and allow it to tick-over on the off-side cylinder only. Then proceed to make the combined adjustment on the R.H. carburettor. Check that the engine runs at the same idling speed on each cylinder.

Again switch off the ignition, replace both h.t. leads, and then start the vertical-twin engine so that it runs on both cylinders. You may now find an undesirable increase in the engine's tick-over speed. If this occurs, unscrew very slightly *both* throttle-stop screws. To ensure an even tick-over it is, of course, essential to lower both throttle valves exactly the same amount for their closed positions.

3. After obtaining good slow-running with both throttle valves resting on their throttle-stop screws, and with the throttle twist-grip fully closed, take up any existing backlash in the air and throttle-valve control cables by means of the adjusters provided mid-way in the cables on single-carburettor models, or at the carburettor end on twin-carburettor models. Fig. 5 shows the adjustment provided. A precise adjustment is *essential* to ensure that *both* throttle valves open exactly the *same* amount and at the same time when the throttle twist-grip is turned anti-clockwise.

To check that the L.H. and R.H. throttle slides (valves) begin to rise *simultaneously*, close the throttle twist-grip completely, poke a finger

OBTAINING GOOD CARBURATION

through each carburettor air intake (with the air filter removed) so that it presses lightly against the throttle slide. Then ask a friend to turn the twist-grip anti-clockwise very gently, and note whether you can feel simultaneous movement upwards from their fully closed (throttle-stop) positions. Should one slide start to rise before the other, correct this difference by means of the control-cable adjusters. There should, by the way, be just perceptible backlash at the twist-grip when both throttle slides are at their lowest positions and in contact with the throttle-stop screws.

Persistent Poor Slow Running. If poor slow running persists after you have carefully adjusted the pilot-air and throttle-stop adjusting screws, consider the possibility of one or more of the following faults—
 1. Obstructed pilot jet(s).
 2. Air leakage through a defective joint between the Amal carburettor flange(s) and the cylinder head.
 3. Air leaks due to excessive wear of the inlet valve guides.
 4. Running with incorrect valve clearances.
 5. An excessively weak mixture caused by badly-seating valves or weak valve springs.
 6. Running with unsuitable type or dirty sparking plugs.
 7. Defective insulation of the h.t. leads attached to the plugs.
 8. Running with incorrect sparking plug and/or contact-breaker gaps.
 9. A faulty battery or battery connection.
 10. A short-circuit in the wiring system.
 11. Incorrect ignition timing.
 12. Heavy carbon deposits in the combustion chambers and on the piston crowns.
 13. A mechanical fault due to wear of the engine components.

An Obstruction in the Pilot Jet. An obstruction in the pilot jet(s) is a likely cause of poor slow running with the carburettor setting and adjustment correct.

On the earlier Amal "Monobloc" type carburettor a detachable pilot jet (*see* Figs. 12, 15) is provided. To remove this jet first remove the external pilot-jet cover nut and then unscrew the pilot jet itself from the carburettor body. In the case of the "Concentric" type carburettor a much smaller detachable pilot jet is provided and its removal necessitates prior removal of the float chamber to render the jet accessible. The float chamber is secured to the carburettor body by two cross-slot screws which are best removed with the Amal service tool provided for this purpose. Removal of the float chamber reveals the small pilot jet projecting downwards from the mating face of the carburettor body.

After removing an obstructed pilot jet from an Amal "Monobloc" or "Concentric" type carburettor, thoroughly clean it with petrol and afterwards have it blown through with a pressure air line. "Concentric" carburettors used on 1969 models do not have a removable pilot jet.

The Jet-needle Position. Should the petrol consumption of an A50 or A65 type B.S.A. twin in good general condition substantially increase after a big mileage, a marked reduction in petrol consumption can often be obtained by *lowering* the tapered jet needle(s), attached to the throttle valve(s), by *one groove*. Leave the jet needle(s) in the new position if marked economy and improved performance result. See that the jet needle clip beds properly home in the needle groove.

Sometimes some slight wear of the needle-jet bore(s) occurs and the only effective remedy is to renew the needle-jet(s). The jet needle, whose tapered end enters each jet, is made of stainless steel and it is therefore not susceptible to wear and renewal.

Excessive Petrol Consumption. Excessive fuel consumption with the carburettor(s) correctly set and adjusted, and not remedied by an alteration in the jet-needle position(s) can be caused by a number of factors, some of which can be quickly dealt with. Here are some possible causes of high consumption: slackness of one or more petrol pipe union-nuts; a leaky petrol tap; a damaged petrol tank seam; leakage from the carburettor due to "flooding" caused by a sticking float needle or faulty float; a loose main or pilot jet; a worn needle jet; a poor joint between the float-chamber cover and float chamber, or between the float chamber and the carburettor body, in the case of a "Monobloc" or "Concentric" carburettor respectively; running with incorrect valve clearances or when the engine needs decarbonizing; poor engine compression due to worn cylinder bores and/or badly-fitting piston rings; running with badly-pitted valves or weak valve springs; late ignition timing; air leaks at the carburettor/cylinder head joint(s); binding of the brake shoes on the brake drums; or a slipping clutch.

Obviously it is not always possible to diagnose the cause of high petrol consumption quickly. But do not attempt to reduce consumption by fitting a smaller-size main jet to one or both carburettors (where two are fitted). Except when a B.S.A. twin is being ridden with the throttle more than half open, an increase in the main jet size will have no effect whatever.

CARBURETTOR MAINTENANCE

Removing Amal Carburettor(s). Close both petrol taps and disconnect the petrol pipes from the carburettor float-chamber(s). On single-carburettor B.S.A. twins both side panels must be removed by turning their snap fasteners and withdrawing the panels from the inlet manifold studs. Twin-carburettor models have no inlet manifold and the side panels are held in position solely by the snap fasteners.

OBTAINING GOOD CARBURATION

On 1966 and later models release the clip(s) shown in Fig. 14 which secure the air filter(s) to the carburettor air intake(s). On 1962-5 models unscrew the filter(s) from the carburettor(s). Then withdraw the air filter(s) downwards between the two ignition coils. Also remove the nuts and washers securing the carburettor(s) to the inlet manifold or cylinder head in the case of single- and twin-carburettor models respectively. If carburettor removal is required only to facilitate dismantling for decarbonizing, do

CARBURETTOR SETTINGS FOR 1962-9 MODELS*

B.S.A. Model	Main Jet	Pilot Jet†	Throttle Valve	Needle Position
A50 "Star" (1962-5)	250	25	$3\frac{1}{2}$	3
A50W "Wasp" (1966)	190	25	$3\frac{1}{2}$	2
A50 "Royal Star" (1966-8)	260	25	$3\frac{1}{2}$	3
A65 "Star" (1962-5)	300	25	$3\frac{1}{2}$	3
A65R "Rocket" (1964-5)	300	25	$3\frac{1}{2}$	3
A50C "Cyclone" (1965)	180	25	$3\frac{1}{2}$	2
A65L "Lightning" (1965)	220	25	$3\frac{1}{2}$	3
A65L "Lightning" (1966-8)	270	25	3	3
A65L "Lightning" (1969)	180	20	3	1
A65H "Hornet" (1966-7)	270	25	3	3
A65T "Thunderbolt" (1966-7)	300	25	$3\frac{1}{2}$	3
A65T "Thunderbolt" (1968-9)	230	20	$3\frac{1}{2}$	1
A65SS "Spitfire" (1966)	250	25	5	3
A65SS "Spitfire" (1967-8)	190	20	3	2
A65ES "Firebird Scrambler" (1968-9)	190	25	$2\frac{1}{2}$	3

* These Amal carburettor settings are those recommended for B.S.A. twins distributed and ridden in the U.K. They do not necessarily apply to corresponding models sold for export.
† The *non-detachable* pilot jet for 1969 models only is No. 622/107.

not bother to disconnect the throttle and air slide (valve) control cables from the carburettor mixing-chamber top, but withdraw the carburettor(s), complete with the control cables, from the manifold or cylinder head studs. Then tie the unit(s) well away from the cylinder head.

To remove the carburettor(s) completely for dismantling, cleaning and inspection, it is desirable to disconnect the throttle and air-control cables at the handlebar end.

To disconnect the throttle-control cable remove the two screws securing the halves of the twist-grip, separate the units and then pull out the cable nipple and withdraw the single or two cables from the twist-grip. To disconnect the air-control cable open the air lever fully; then close it and simultaneously pull the outer casing and the cable from the stop, remove the nipple from the air lever, and pull from the frame clips the throttle and air-control cables. Complete carburettor removal is now possible.

Dismantling Amal Carburettor(s). The dismantling procedure is similar for "Monobloc" and "Concentric" type carburettors, but there are some variations in procedure, mainly with regard to the jets and the float chamber whose design and layout differ.

On twin-carburettor models the two air-control cables from the carburettors are connected at a junction box to a single cable for the air lever. Removal of the cables from the carburettors should present no difficulty

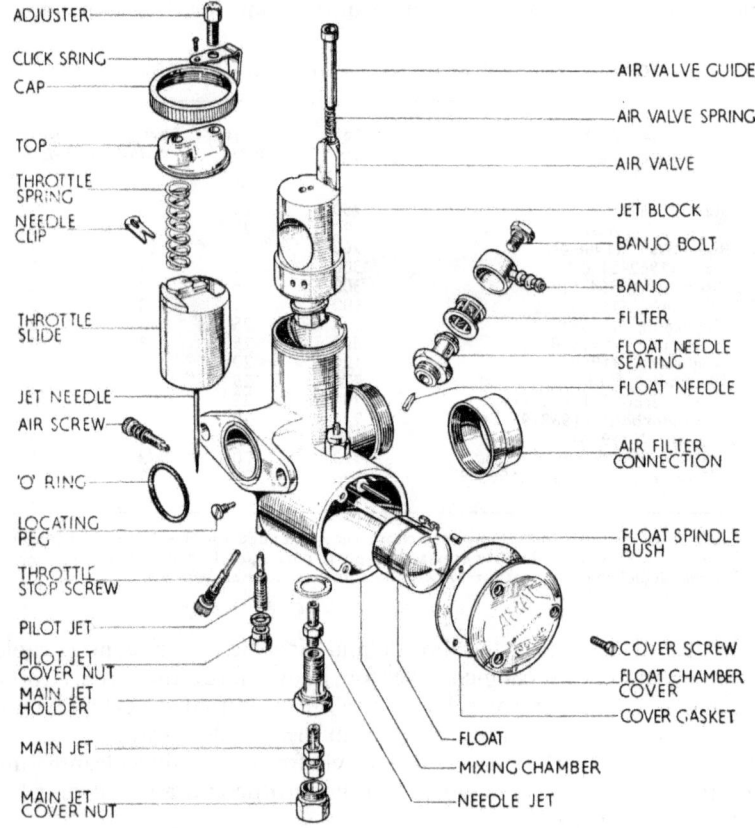

Fig 15 Exploded view of Amal "Monobloc" type carburettor

This carburettor, with an integral float chamber, is fitted to all 1962–6 models except the 654 c.c Model A65SS.
(B.S.A. Workshop Manual)

after the two cables have been disconnected from the throttle twist-grip and the single cable from the air lever.

Referring to Figs. 15, 16, proceed with the dismantling of the Amal carburettor or each of the two Amal carburettors in the following manner.

OBTAINING GOOD CARBURATION

Remove the mixing-chamber top (secured by a knurled cap and click-spring on a "Monobloc," and by two screws on a "Concentric" carburettor) and withdraw the throttle and air slides (valves) from the mixing chamber. Now remove the spring clip[1] which secures the tapered jet needle to the throttle slide, compress the latter's return spring, and then push the cable nipple down and out of the slide. To free the air slide, compress its return spring and slide the cable nipple from the base of the air slide.

On a "monobloc" carburettor (*see* Fig. 14) unscrew the three slotted screws and withdraw the vertical cover and washer from the float chamber which is integral with the carburettor body. This gives access to the float spindle bush, the hinged float, and its triangular-section moulded-nylon needle. Lay all these parts in a safe place for cleaning and inspection. Unscrew the banjo bolt securing the top-feed petrol pipe banjo connection to the float-needle seating block, and proceed to remove the banjo, the fine-gauze cylindrical filter, and the top-feed union washer. Also unscrew the float-needle seating block and the tickler assembly which, by the way, embodies the float-chamber vent. Then withdraw the tickler and its spring.

The Amal "Concentric" type carburettor (*see* Fig. 16) has a float chamber entirely different from that of the "Monobloc" type and it is detachable from the body of the carburettor instead of being integral with it. It can be removed after unscrewing two cross-slot screws. To facilitate dismantling and assembling the "Concentric" type carburettor, a useful service tool can be obtained from any Amal spares stockist. It comprises a main-jet box spanner and tommy-bar with cross-slot screwdriver ends, one of them being angled for float chamber removal. The contents of the float chamber are, a hinged concentric float with forked arm, a pivot for the latter, and a float needle of different type from that used in the float chamber of the "Monobloc" instrument. Unlike the "Monobloc" design, the float chamber has a *bottom* petrol-feed with a banjo bolt and cylindrical fine-gauze filter. Dismantling should present no problem, but handle the rather delicate contents of the float chamber with care.

After removing the contents from the float chamber of a "Monobloc" type carburettor, proceed to remove the pilot-air adjusting screw and the throttle-stop screw, followed by the main jet, the main-jet holder and the needle jet. Remove the jet block locating-screw to the left of and slightly below the pilot-air adjusting screw. Then push or tap out (with a small wooden handle or mallet) the jet block and its fibre seal through and out of the large end of the carburettor body. To remove the pilot jet it is only necessary to remove the pilot-jet cover nut and then unscrew the jet itself.

---

[1] The latest Amal "Concentric" type carburettor has a horseshoe-shaped spring clip which enables the jet needle to be extracted from the throttle slide, it desired, without first having to detach the throttle cable. This improved spring clip also makes it easier to fit the throttle slide to the end of the operating cable.

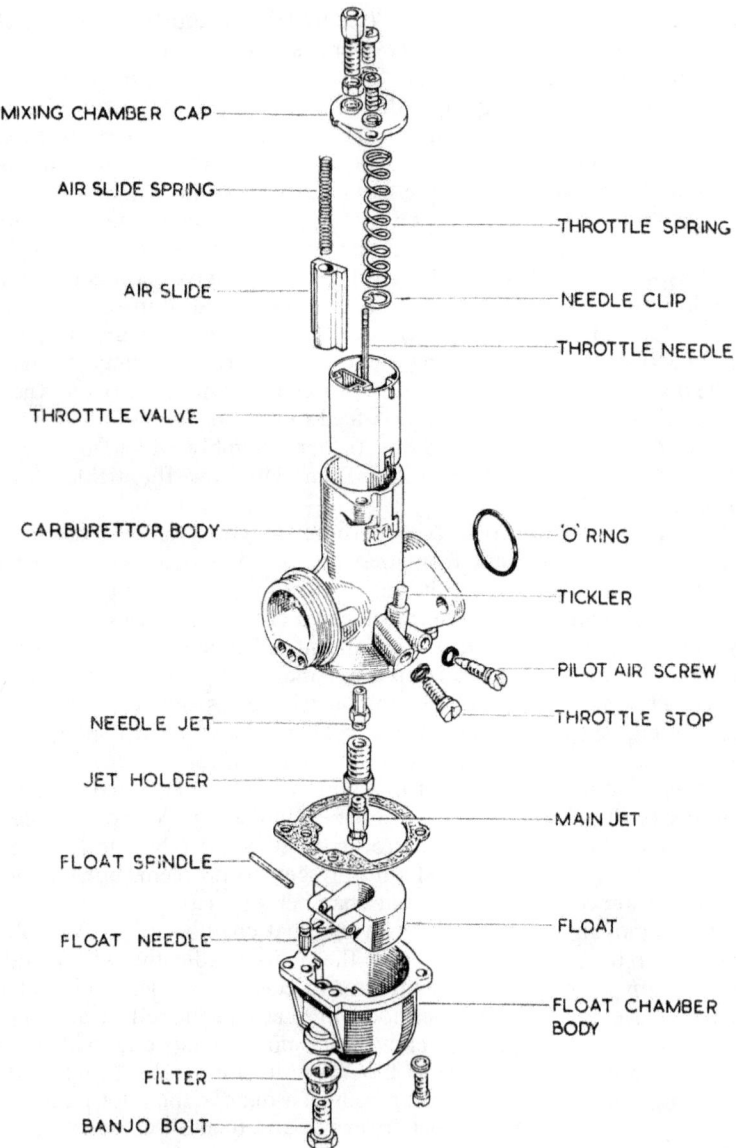

Fig 16 Exploded view of Amal "Concentric" type carburettor

This redesigned Amal instrument, fitted to some 1967, all 1968–9 models, and the 1967–8 654 c.c. Model A65SS, differs from the "Monobloc" type shown in Fig. 15 mainly in that it has bottom petrol feed, a new detachable concentric float chamber and an altered jet arrangement.
(B.S.A. Workshop Manual)

OBTAINING GOOD CARBURATION

On a "concentric" type Amal carburettor main and pilot jet removal (see Figs. 15, 16) is similar to removal procedure for a "Monobloc" type instrument, but cannot for obvious reasons be effected until the float-chamber unit has been removed as previously described. Also in this case there is no main jet cover-nut to be unscrewed prior to removing the main jet, the main-jet holder, and the small needle jet. The main jet should be removed with the Amal box spanner and tommy-bar previously mentioned, and the removal of the pilot jet necessitates using a very small screwdriver of the type commonly used for tightening screws in electrical work. As mentioned on an earlier page, "Concentric" type carburettors fitted to 1969 models do not have a removable pilot jet.

Note that rubber "O" rings are used on the flanged attachment faces of both "Monobloc" and "Concentric" type Amal carburettors, and in the case of the latter type instrument also on the shanks of the throttle-stop and pilot-air adjusting screws. It is desirable to renew all these "O" rings during the assembly of the carburettor(s) and prior to replacement on the power unit.

Cleaning Amal Carburettor Components. Wash *all* the components thoroughly clean with petrol and blow through the various ducts and passages to ensure that they are unobstructed. Pay special attention to the pilot-jet feed and air passages and also to the main and pilot jets. When drying the various components avoid using a fluffy rag. Remove for thorough cleaning the cylindrical gauze filter positioned inside the top or bottom feed-pipe banjo in the case of the "Monobloc" or "Concentric" float chamber respectively.

Inspecting the Components. After dismantling an Amal "Monobloc" or "Concentric" carburettor which has been in continuous service for a very considerable time, it is desirable to inspect closely its various components. The inspection for a single carburettor or each of twin carburettors should include the following—

1. *The Carburettor Flange.* Sometimes slight distortion of the attachment flange occurs and this is likely to cause air leaks. Check the flange face for truth with a straight-edge. If the face is found to be slightly concave, have it ground down on a garage grinder or, if you are sufficiently skilled, true up the face with a file and some fine-grade emery-cloth laid flat on a surface plate until the face becomes dead flat and smooth. If not in perfect condition, renew its rubber "O" ring.

2. *The Throttle Valve.* Check this slide for fit in the mixing chamber and for wear of its rear face. Should appreciable play be observed, renew the slide immediately, being careful to see that the new slide has the correct degree of cut-away. Also verify that the throttle-valve return spring has not lost its normal compressive strength.

3. *The Air Valve.* Examine this slide for excessive wear and scoring.

See that its surface has not worn right through at any point. The slide should be a really good fit in the jet block and its return spring must have adequate compressive strength. Inspect its coils for signs of wear.

4. *The Needle Jet and Jet Needle.* Inspect the jet and the tapered end of the jet needle for wear or possible scoring. The spring clip securing the tapered needle to the throttle valve (slide) must grip the jet needle firmly. Free rotation must not occur as this is liable to cause wear of the needle groove. It is, of course, important that the spring clip enters the groove recommended by the makers.

5. *The Jet Block.* Verify by blowing that the pilot-jet ducts are quite clear and that the jet-block fibre seal on the "Monobloc" carburettor is in perfect condition.

6. *The Float Chamber.* See that its inside is scrupulously clean and free of any deposits or impurities. Examine *all* its components most carefully and verify that the air vent is unobstructed. The hinged float must be free from any damage or leakage. Shake it to make sure it contains no petrol. Also scrutinize the hinge components and the small moulded-nylon needle and the valve seating. The needle must be absolutely undamaged and clean. On a "Monobloc" type carburettor with integral float chamber, renew the washer for its cover if damaged in any way, otherwise petrol leakage will later occur.

7. *The Petrol Filter.* Check the condition of the cylindrical fine-gauze filter which fits inside the banjo for the top or bottom petrol-pipe connection. Make certain that the gauze is quite clean and that at no point has it parted from its supporting structure.

Assembling Amal Carburettors. The assembly of a "Monobloc" or "Concentric" type Amal carburettor, or two carburettors, should present no special difficulty, but a few important points which should be noted are as follows—

1. Do not use again any rubber, fibre or paper washers unless found to be in perfect condition. Renew *all* unserviceable washers before commencing to assemble the carburettor(s).

2. When replacing the jet block on a "Monobloc" carburettor, see that the fibre washer is first positioned as indicated in Fig. 15. Also verify that the locating-peg screwed into the carburettor body aligns with the locating slot in the jet block. Push or tap home the latter from the upper end of the mixing chamber.

3. When replacing the throttle valve (the slide) in the body of a "Concentric" carburettor, make sure that the jet needle engages properly with the needle jet. Make quite sure that the lower end of the jet needle actually enters the jet tube.

4. When assembling a "Concentric" carburettor always make certain that the spring clip engages the correct jet-needle groove and that the clip lies flat against the inside base of the throttle valve.

OBTAINING GOOD CARBURATION

5. On a "Concentric" carburettor with the latest horse-shoe shaped spring-clip securing the jet needle to the throttle valve it is possible to couple the cable nipple to the socket in the throttle slide and then hold up the spring clip with the fingers and slip the jet needle into position with the needle-clip attached. Then release the spring to ensure that its lower end is holding the needle-clip flat against the inside base of the throttle slide.

6. With a "Monobloc" or "Concentric" type carburettor, before replacing the pilot-air and throttle-stop adjusting screws, do not forget to fit the locking springs or small "O" rings respectively.

7. On a "Monobloc" instrument be sure that the float-spindle bush fits on the *outer* end of the spindle and that the pressure-pad is at the *top* to allow the moulded-nylon needle to rest on it. Also fit the gasket between the joint of the integral float chamber and its cover. The joint face and the gasket must be undamaged and the three cover-securing screws must be tightened *evenly* and firmly to ensure a petrol-tight joint.

8. When replacing the detachable float-chamber on a "Concentric" carburettor (*see* Fig. 16) check that the ends of the float hinge-pin are properly seated in their sockets and not partly resting on the flange face. If the end of a hinge-pin stands proud of its socket and rests on the flange, severe flooding is likely and the carburettor body and/or float chamber may become damaged.

Also see that the extension of the float grips the neck of the float needle properly. Be sure to fit the float-chamber gasket the right way round to ensure correct alignment of its two rear holes with the jet passages in the float-chamber casting. Faulty replacement of this gasket will cause flooding to occur.

9. Before the attachment of a "Monobloc" or "Concentric" carburettor to the manifold or cylinder head, make sure that a new "O" ring (which is narrower on the "Concentric" instrument) is pressed fully home into the flange groove all round and that it does not overlap anywhere. After fitting the carburettor-flange gasket(s) and positioning the carburettor flange over the manifold or cylinder-head securing studs, tighten down *absolutely evenly* the two securing nuts.

THE AIR FILTERS

A "pill-box" type air filter is screwed or clipped to the air intake(s) of the single or twin carburettors of most 1962–9 A50 and A65 type B.S.A. vertical twins. The provision of an air filter does, by the way, determine the correct jet setting for a carburettor; therefore if for some reason you ride your mount without its air filter or filters be careful not to allow its engine to become overheated by running on an excessively weak mixture. Careful testing by means of the air valve (slide) should indicate whether a larger main jet and/or higher needle-jet position is necessary.

Dismantling, Cleaning and Assembling. Removal of the air filter(s) from the carburettor(s) is referred to on page 31. To dismantle and clean a filter, proceed as follows. Unscrew the nut and bolt securing the ends of the perforated metal-band. Now open out the band sufficiently to permit the complete air filter assembly to be dismantled as shown in Fig. 17. Then wash the element thoroughly in petrol and afterwards dry it. A felt element was used on 1962–5 models, but all 1966 and later models have "surgical gauze" elements.

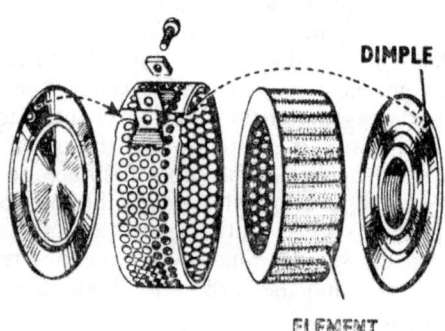

Fig 17   An air filter shown dismantled

The arrows indicate correct end-plate "dimple" location. On 1968 and later models these "dimples" are omitted, and on 1966–9 models the front end-plate is not threaded for filter attachment to the carburettor air intake. A clip fixing (see Fig. 14) is used.

Assemble the air filter(s) in the reverse order of dismantling and make quite sure that the rubber ring between the filter and carburettor is (where specified) replaced. If its condition is suspect, renew the ring immediately. When assembling the air filter on a 1962–3 model it is important to see that the "dimples" impressed on its front and rear end-plates locate as indicated in Fig. 17 at the joint of the perforated metal band. This ensures that the air filter unit (1964–5 models) rotates as a complete unit when it is screwed on to the carburettor air-intake. On later air filters of the screw-on type the above-mentioned "dimples" are omitted.

When replacing an air filter on the air intake of an carburettor fitted to 1962–5 B.S.A. models be very careful not to "cross" the threads on the intake of the carburettor which is made of comparatively soft metal. All 1966 and later models have a clip method of air-filter attachment.

3 Correct Lubrication

This chapter contains fully comprehensive instructions for the correct lubrication of *all* 1962–9 A50 and A65 type B.S.A. vertical twins. The engines of all these models have full dry-sump lubrication which normally requires little maintenance. This maintenance, however, and the correct lubrication at regular intervals of various motor-cycle components, are *vitally* important to ensure maximum performance and the minimum trouble and expense.

ENGINE LUBRICATION

The B.S.A. Dry Sump System. The "heart" of this D.S. system (*see* Fig. 18) is a double-gear type oil pump housed low down within the timing case. One set of gears in the pump assembly draws engine oil from the oil tank through a cylindrical gauze filter in the tank itself (*see* Fig. 20) and through the oil supply pipe, and then pressure-feeds oil past a non-return valve to the timing-side main bearing of the crankshaft, through drillings in this crankshaft, on past a sludge trap, and on to the connecting-rod big-end bearings. From here oil is thrown off by centrifugal force on to the walls of the two cylinder bores and also on to the gudgeon-pin bearings. Some of the oil is circulated through ducts and special reservoirs to lubricate the camshaft, timing gears, etc.

On 1969 models only, an oil-pressure warning light is fitted on the headlamp where it is visible while riding. It should always remain extinguished while the engine is running. Stop at once if the light appears, otherwise serious harm will be done to the engine. Do not start up again until the reason for the failure of oil pressure is found and rectified.

An oil-pressure release valve (located as shown by the inset in Fig. 18) opens when engine r.p.m. rise to about 3,000 r.p.m. and the oil pressure begins to exceed about 50 lb per sq in. This causes excess oil to be released direct into the oil sump from where it is returned to the oil tank via the pump through the oil-return pipe. The thread on this component was changed to the "unified" form for the 1969 season and is not interchangeable with those on earlier models.

After thoroughly lubricating the many moving parts of the engine, the oil drains down through another gauze filter in the bottom of the crankcase (*see* Fig. 22) to a small sump bolted to the underside of the crankcase.

A second and larger set of gears in the pump assembly draws oil past the pump ball valve (*see* Fig. 22) and pumps it back through the oil-return pipe up to the oil tank and at a greater rate than the smaller capacity gears drawing oil through the oil-supply pipe down to the crankshaft. The effect of this difference is that no flooding of the oil sump ever occurs and a full dry-sump system is obtained.

The overhead-rocker mechanism is automatically lubricated by a low-pressure feed pipe connected between the oil-return pipe (near its tank end or at the crankcase union from 1967 onwards) and the rocker-box which is integral with the cylinder head. The pipe union at this end is above the carburettor intake as indicated in Fig 18. The oil by-passed from the return pipe (*see* Fig 20) to the rocker-box is then pressure-fed through drillings to the inlet and exhaust rocker spindles, the ball-ended rocker pins, and the valve-clearance adjuster screws. A split pin at the base of the central pillar meters the oil feed to the rockers.

After lubricating the whole of the overhead-rocker mechanism, oil from the rocker-box drains down into the oil sump through the tunnel provided for the push-rods. During its downwards passage the four tappets are effectively lubricated. The oil pump, by the way, has no adjustment, and there is no regulator for altering the oil pressure.

Seven Important Points. There are seven important points to note with regard to the correct lubrication of a 499 c.c. or 654 c.c. B.S.A. vertical-twin engine. These are as follows—

1. Always run-in a new or reconditioned (rebored) engine with the utmost care for 1,500 miles. Impatience during the early life of an engine can be most expensive.

2. Keep the union nuts for the oil-supply pipe, the oil-return pipe, and the by-pass for the rocker-box securely tightened to prevent any oil leakage. Also see that no leakage occurs at the crankcase, timing-case cover and rocker-box joints.

3. Always keep the oil tank replenished to the correct level with a recommended brand of engine oil of the correct grade.

4. Frequently check that the engine oil *is* circulating properly.

5. While running-in an engine, change the oil in the tank at 250, 500 and 1,000 mile intervals, and subsequently every 2,000 miles.

6. When changing the engine oil always thoroughly clean the cylindrical gauze filter attached to the tank drain plug.

7. Clean the crankcase gauze filter every 2,000 miles and check the efficiency of the non-return ball valve.

Running-in an Engine. Comprehensive advice about properly running-in a new or reconditioned (rebored) engine, why this is so essential, points to watch during running-in, and some maintenance attention of special importance during the running-in period of 1,500 miles, are given on pages 21–2.

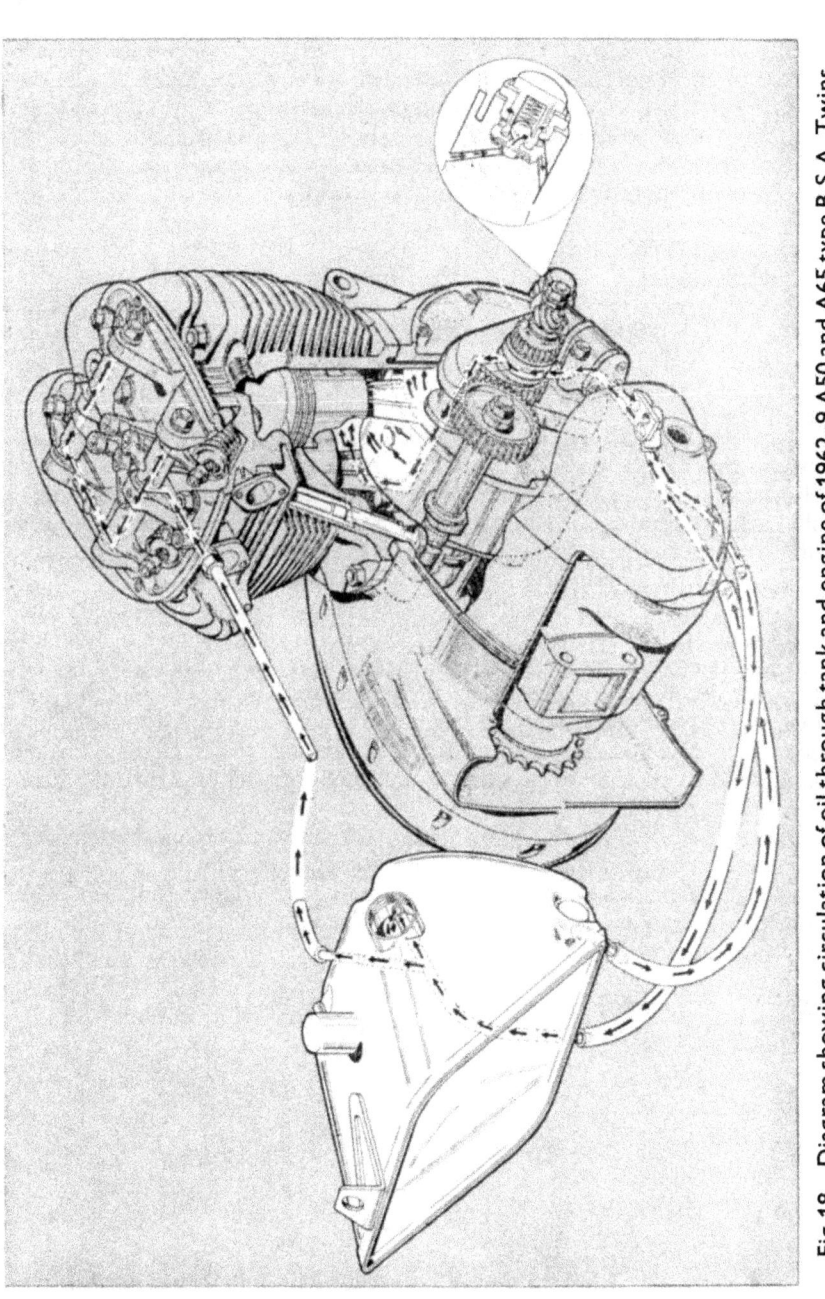

Fig 18 Diagram showing circulation of oil through tank and engine of 1962–9 A50 and A65 type B.S.A. Twins
(*B.S.A. Workshop Manual*)

Recommended Engine Oils. Never run a B.S.A. engine on an inferior brand of engine oil or on a recommended brand of unsuitable grade. To ensure easy starting, the best performance at all throttle openings, and the minimum wear of engine components, always replenish the oil tank with one of the following six brands and grades of engine oil recommended after exhaustive tests by B.S.A. Motor Cycles Ltd.—

1. Castrol GTX.
2. Mobil Super.
3. Shell Super 100.
4. B.P. Energol Visco-Static 20W/50.
5. Esso Uniflo.
6. Texaco Havoline 20W/50.

Note that the above engine oil recommendations are not tabulated in any order of priority. All of them are excellent for use in *temperate* climates, but in no circumstances mix two different brands, otherwise some sludge formation is probable and this is liable to damage the B.S.A. power unit. If some sludge accumulates, flush out the tank with paraffin. Remove all traces of paraffin before replenishing the tank.

For the above-stated reason, B.S.A. oil (U.S.A. only) should never be topped-up with a detergent oil. Where riding is undertaken in countries having extremes of temperature, a higher or lower S.A.E. number may be required according to whether the air temperature is abnormally high or low respectively. When buying engine oil, always make a point of purchasing it in sealed cans or from branded cabinets. When changing from one brand to another, always first completely drain the oil tank and flush it out with paraffin.

Replenishing Oil Tank. Always keep the oil tank replenished to the recommended level. All 1966–9 models have a combined filler cap and dipstick, the latter indicating the *safe* maximum and minimum oil levels. On some earlier models the correct level is marked on the outside of the oil tank. Obviously the more oil there is in circulation, the cooler it is and the smaller is the chance of its becoming quickly unserviceable. For these reasons it is desirable as far as possible to keep the oil at or close to the *maximum* safe level.

Warming Up a Cold B.S.A. Engine. Do this at a *moderate* speed when the motor-cycle is stationary for the several good reasons explained on page 17. After warming up the engine, before take-off always make a quick check that the engine oil is circulating properly at normal pressure by observing the continuous ejection of oil (and air bubbles) from the end of the oil-return pipe. If no ejection occurs, stop the engine immediately and investigate the cause, possibly faulty non-return ball valve.

Changing the Engine Oil and Cleaning Tank Filter. Change the engine oil and clean the cylindrical gauze tank-filter with the engine *warm* after a run in the following manner.

CORRECT LUBRICATION 43

To obtain access to the tank drain-plug and integral gauze-filter remove the detachable side panel from the offside of the motor-cycle (*see* Fig. 19). On a single-carburettor B.S.A. release the snap fastener(s) and pull the side panel from the carburettor inlet-manifold stud or other connection.

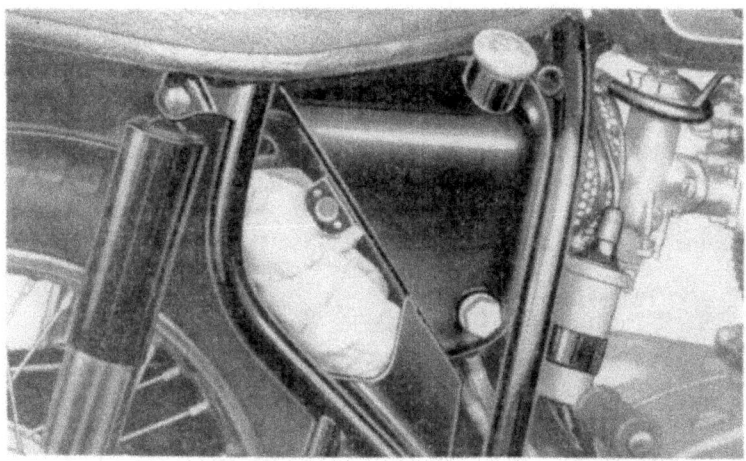

Fig 19 An early single-carburettor B.S.A. Twin with side panel removed giving access to the rubber-mounted oil tank and its combined drain plug and filter unit

Removal of the off-side panel also gives immediate access to the tool-kit, the Amal "Monobloc" carburettor, the Vokes air filter and the ignition coil.

In the case of a twin-carburettor model with a side panel of different shape to that fitted to single-carburettor models a carburettor securing stud is not used as a panel anchorage point.

Having removed the off-side panel, unscrew the combined drain plug and gauze filter (R.H. thread) fitted to the front bottom corner of the oil tank, as shown in Figs. 19, 20, 21, close to the oil-supply pipe. Then drain off the whole of the used oil into a suitable receptacle. To assist draining straight into this receptacle it is advisable to make up a small chute from some cardboard or sheet metal. Tilt the motor-cycle slightly over to the right to ensure that no oil is left inside the tank.

If for any reason (*see* page 42) the oil tank contains appreciable sludge, flush the tank out thoroughly with paraffin after disconnecting the oil-supply pipe from the tank to the oil pump. See that all trace of paraffin is subsequently removed.

Clean the cylindrical gauze-filter very thoroughly in petrol and before fitting the drain plug/filter unit to the tank make sure that the gauze filter is quite dry and undamaged. When drying it on no account use a fluffy rag. Also check that the fibre joint-washer is in perfect condition. If it is not, renew it immediately. Then screw home firmly the drain plug/filter unit to ensure an absolutely oil-tight joint. Afterwards carefully position the off-side panel, first inserting the front connection where carburettor-stud attachment is provided. Secure in position by the snap fastener(s). Finally replenish the oil tank with a recommended brand and grade of engine oil as previously described.

After changing the engine oil, always remove and clean the crankcase gauze-filter. A brief run-up of the engine to normal tick-over speed will then, after a short period, show whether normal oil circulation occurs, indicated by an intermittent flow of oil from the end of the return pipe.

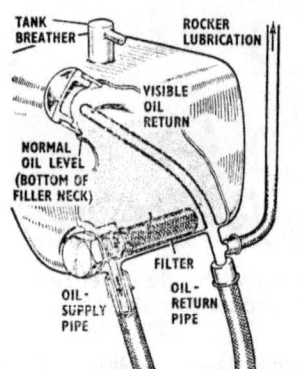 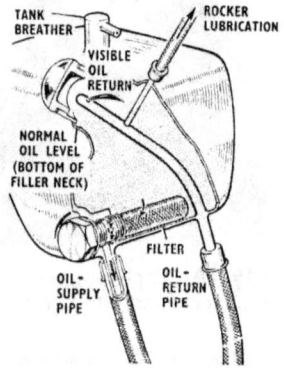

Figs 20, 21   Diagrams showing (left) the 1962–3 oil tank, and (right) the 1964–9 version, and associated oil pipes, etc.

Note the external and internal attachment of the by-pass pipe for overhead rocker lubrication in the case of the earlier and later tanks respectively. The filler-cap on all 1966–9 models has a dip-stick (not shown), and on all 1962–9 models the oil-return pipes cross over.

Cleaning the Crankcase Filter. As may be seen in Fig. 22, the large-diameter gauze filter is integral with the rectangular oil sump, the unit being secured to the under side of the crankcase and readily detachable for cleaning as follows.

Unscrew in a diagonal order and remove the four nuts from the crank-case studs, remove the four shake-proof or spring washers, and then withdraw the combined oil sump and gauze filter, and also the joint washer. Allow all oil to drain from the crankcase into a suitable receptacle. Invert the detachable filter/sump unit and also drain off all oil from this. Afterwards thoroughly clean the unit with petrol, being careful not to use a fluffy rag to clean the gauze filter.

Before replacing the unit on the crankcase face make sure that all petrol has evaporated from it, that its joint face and the corresponding

CORRECT LUBRICATION 45

crankcase face are absolutely clean, and that the joint washer is quite undamaged. Renew this washer if not in perfect condition. Also check that the pump suction-pipe non-return ball valve is fully operational. This ball valve, shown in Fig. 22, is referred to in more detail in a later paragraph. To assist the pump to "prime," it is advisable to add ½ pint of engine oil to the crankcase before starting up. The easiest way is to remove the timing plug on the front of the crankcase, Fig. 40, and pour the oil in through the exposed hole. Operate the starter pedal twenty or thirty times

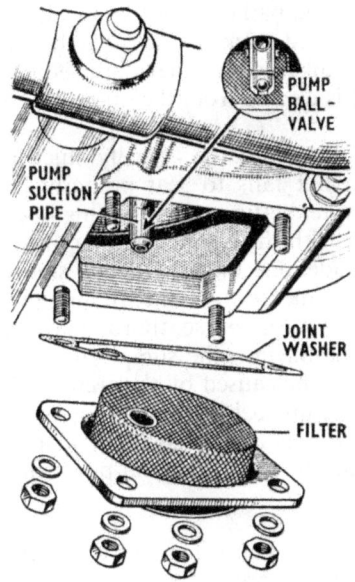

Fig 22 Underneath of B.S.A. crankcase with filter/sump unit removed for cleaning

The location of the pump suction-pipe and its internal non-return ball valve are also shown. On some earlier models "star"-shaped shake-proof washers, instead of the four spring-washers shown, were used to secure the filter/sump unit retaining nuts.

with the ignition switched off until oil is seen returning to the tank. Do not forget to allow sufficient space in the tank to receive this oil which will, in due course, be cleared from the crankcase.

When assembling the filter/sump unit, apply some jointing compound to the mating joint faces, replace the joint washer, the unit, the four shakeproof or spring washers, and the four securing nuts. To avoid any risk of slight distortion, and to ensure an absolutely oil-tight joint, tighten the four nuts evenly and firmly, and preferably in a diagonal order.

The Pump Suction-pipe Non-return Valve. As may also be observed in Fig. 22, removal of the crankcase filter/sump unit exposes the end of the pump suction-pipe and the small internal ball-valve adjoining its orifice. When you remove the filter/sump unit for thorough cleaning always make a point of checking that the ball of the valve is quite free and not stuck on its seating. Insert a length of wire through the suction-pipe orifice, push the ball up and off its seating and afterwards check that when released the ball drops back on its seating through its own weight; if it fails this test it is likely that some sludge has accumulated inside the pump suction-pipe, and must be carefully cleaned out.

If the above-mentioned ball *adheres* to its seating it becomes impossible for any oil to be pumped back to the tank through the oil-return pipe, and flooding of the crankcase is an inevitable sequel. Immediately consider this trouble if no oil is ejected from the oil-return pipe while the engine is running.

If a ball valve has not become actually stuck on its seating through sludge accumulation but fails to seat properly because of sludge or a particle of foreign matter getting on the seating, there may be an oil return indicated at the tank with the engine running, but when the engine is left stationary for a considerable time oil slowly siphons into the sump and clouds of blue smoke emerge from the exhaust pipes when the engine is re-started. The remedy is, of course, thorough cleaning.

Siphoning of engine oil into the sump, giving results similar to those just described, can also be caused by the second of the non-return valves (provided in the engine just behind the oil-pump body) failing to function effectively, although this is much less likely than with the first valve. In this case it is necessary to remove the oil pump in order to diagnose and remedy the trouble.

The Oil-pressure Release Valve. This valve, associated with engine r.p.m. referred to on page 39, is pre-set for pressure by B.S.A. Motor Cycles Ltd. during final assembly and testing; it is unwise to alter the maker's original setting. However, after a very considerable mileage has been covered, some weakness and corrosion of the pressure spring may develop. The former causes a reduction in the free length of the spring which should be 0·609 in. The latter usually indicates that the spring and ball must both be renewed.

To remove the oil-pressure release valve, unscrew its large hexagon; to dismantle it, afterwards unscrew the small hexagon. Do not remove the gauze filter provided, and make quite sure that all the fibre washers are fit for further service. All later B.S.A. twins have "O" rings fitted instead of fibre washers.

The Oil-supply and Oil-return Pipes. If for any reason you disconnect and remove these two pipes (*see* Figs. 18, 20) from the oil tank and crank-case, it is vitally important to reconnect the pipes, as shown in Fig. 18,

CORRECT LUBRICATION

so that they cross over. The oil-supply pipe (the *outer* one at the tank) must be attached to the *inner* crankcase connection. Failure to re-connect the pipes correctly results in the oil pump drawing in *air* through the oil-return pipe. This is extremely bad for the engine!

Pipe removal is quite simple, a single bolt securing both of them by a union plate to the crankcase at a point slightly to the off side of the oil sump filter. On earlier B.S.A. twins a plain paper washer was used for the joint, but all later models have two rubber "O" rings fitted. This ensures a perfect oil seal and the earlier arrangement can be altered in the event of oil leakage occurring, but this requires the fitting of two *new* pipes. Flexible pipe attachments and not union nuts are specified for the tank ends of both pipes.

When reconnecting the one-piece oil pipe union-plate to the crankcase face, on earlier models fit a new paper washer and smear the joint faces sparingly with some jointing compound. On later B.S.A. models provided with two rubber "O" rings instead of a paper washer, do not apply any jointing compound.

The Double-gear Oil Pump. This B.S.A. pump has no *adjustment* and is of very robust design. No trouble should normally be experienced with it, provided the engine oil is kept clean, until an extremely big mileage has been covered.

Should pump trouble eventually develop or be suspected, remove the oil pump from the crankcase and also take out the non-return valve ball and spring (located behind the pump body). Then dismantle the pump itself. Lever up the circlip at the spindle end and extract it with a small pair of pliers. The thrust washer and spindle can now be removed. Then remove the four screws from the base of the pump, and withdraw the base plate and spindle housing. This exposes the two pairs of gears. Wash all pump components very thoroughly in petrol, allow them to dry and then closely inspect the parts for evidence of something causing the pump trouble and poor oil circulation.

When inspecting the pump components, look for the following: a faulty non-return valve ball and/or spring; foreign matter jammed between gear teeth, or metal particles embedded in the teeth of one or more gears (*see* Fig. 23); deep score marks in the pump body; wear of the pump-spindle teeth; and the condition of the "O" ring fitted between the feed driving-gear and the pump-spindle housing (on later models).

Reduced Oil Pressure. A big reduction in normal oil pressure (40–45 lb per sq in.) can be most damaging to the engine because it necessarily involves a big reduction in the amount of oil delivered by the oil pump to the power unit. It is, of course, usually diagnosed by a marked reduction in the amount of oil ejected from the return-pipe orifice while the engine

is running. Should no oil ejection occur, stop the engine *immediately*. Possible causes of a marked reduction in oil pressure are—
1. The level of oil inside the tank is too low (*see* page 42).
2. Incorrect attachment of the oil-supply and oil-return pipes (*see* page 44).
3. Dirty oil tank and/or crankcase filter(s), causing an obstruction in the oil circulation system.
4. Serious wear of, or damage to, oil-pump components.
5. Badly worn connecting-rod big-end bearing shells.
6. One or more external oil leakages.

The Contact-breaker and Auto-advance Unit. These require slight, but nevertheless important, lubrication about every 5,000 miles, i.e. when

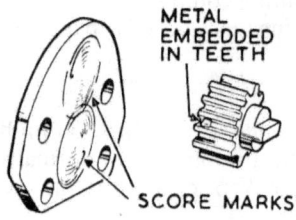

Fig 23   Two possible causes of pump trouble after prolonged use

The double-gear pump has, of course, two pairs of gears, one pair of which (on the return side) has considerably greater pumping capacity than the other pair.
(B.S.A. Workshop Manual)

cleaning and if necessary adjusting the contacts of the contact-breaker. To obtain access to a Lucas type 4CA or 6CA (on 1968–9 models) contact-breaker assembly, and the automatic ignition advance-and-retard mechanism behind the contact-breaker back plate, is simple; remove the circular metal cover, shown at 8 in Fig. 10, from the outer timing cover of your vertical twin.

Apply a *very small* amount of thin grease, or engine oil, to the felt pad provided for cam lubrication (*see* Fig. 37). Be most careful not to apply excessive lubricant, otherwise difficult starting and some misfiring may result from some of the lubricant getting on one or both sets of contacts. Also slowly rotate the engine until the cam slot is uppermost as shown in Fig. 36 and apply to it *one spot* of clean engine oil so as to lubricate the cam spindle, and also another spot of oil to each of the two rocker-arm pivot posts shown in Fig. 36.

On 1969 models, the spindle is treated with a special dry lubricant and *oil must not be applied* otherwise the cam will tend to seize on its bearing.

To obtain access to the auto-advance unit mounted behind the contact-breaker plate, remove the two plate securing screws (*see* Fig. 36) and

CORRECT LUBRICATION

withdraw the backplate complete with contacts, capacitors, etc. The latter are mounted elsewhere on the machine on later models. Do *not* remove the cam's central securing bolt, otherwise the ignition will require to be re-timed. When checking the bob-weights for free movement, lubricate their bearings with a drop of *thin* oil. For the sake of the contacts, beware of excessive lubrication here and at all other lubrication points.

After replacing the contact-breaker backplate, check the ignition timing and make an adjustment as required by slightly re-setting the plate (*see*

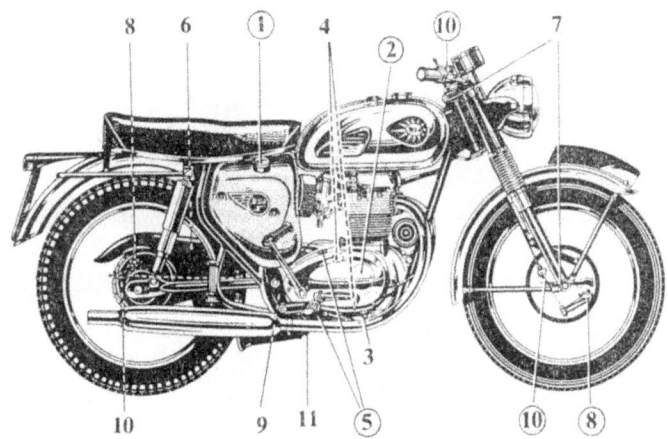

Fig 24 Lubrication chart showing location of most items requiring attention on 1962–9 B.S.A. type A50 and A65 O.H.V. Vertical Twins

On all 1963–5 "Star" models and on the 1964–5 A65R "Rockets" the rear brake rod is on the off side of the machine and is actuated by a brake cross-shaft which requires occasional greasing (see page 55). The wheel hubs and steering head bearings on all models have no grease nipples fitted and only require repacking with grease at 12,000 mile intervals. Do not forget the sidecar chassis where a sidecar is attached. Note that the numbers within circles apply to items on the right side of the motor-cycle.

page 74). Finally replace and firmly secure the circular cover to the outer timing cover. On 1968–9 models, the gaps are independently adjustable (*see* page 74).

Oil Seal for Contact-breaker Unit. Note that the contact-breaker and auto-advance unit is operated from the intermediate timing gear and is housed in a separate compartment. This has a judiciously placed shield to prevent any engine oil getting on to the contacts of the contact-breaker. Should frequent oiling-up of the contacts develop, suspect a faulty shield; fit a new one with its lip (bearing on the cam shaft) facing *towards* the crankcase interior.

Key to Fig 24

Item No.	Description of Item	Lubrication, etc., required	See page
1	Oil tank	Keep oil level correct; change engine oil and clean tank filter every 2,000 miles	42
2	Contact-breaker and auto-advance unit	Grease or oil slightly every 5,000 miles	48
3	Crankcase filter	Clean every 2,000 miles	44
4	Gearbox	Replenish to correct oil level every 2,000 miles; drain and refill every 5,000 miles	50, 51
5	Primary chain	Check level of oil in oil-bath every 1,000 miles and top-up as required; drain and refill every 5,000 miles	52
6	Secondary chain	Keep oil-bath for primary chain topped-up to correct level; periodically remove chain, thoroughly clean and immerse in warm graphite grease	53
7	Telescopic front forks	Drain and refill with oil every 10,000 miles	54
8, 9	Front and rear brakes	Every 2,000 miles grease cam spindles and cross-shaft (where fitted); also oil brake-pedal pivot	55
10	Control lever, exposed cables and joints	Every 2,000 miles oil or grease as required	57
11	Central-stand pivot	Grease every 2,000 miles	58

MOTOR-CYCLE ITEMS

Do not be very kind to your engine but indifferent to the many important items comprising the motor-cycle in which your engine is installed.

Replenish Gearbox to Correct Oil Level Every 2,000 *Miles.* The constant-mesh B.S.A. gearbox is quite independent of the engine for its lubrication and has a separate housing and oil-bath formed in unit construction with the crankcase. A stand-pipe (*see* Fig. 25) is built in with the drain plug, and when topping-up the gearbox to the correct oil level the drain plug must always be left in position. A dip-stick, attached to the gearbox filler cap, supersedes the standpipe for 1968–9 models.

Checking the oil level necessarily involves the addition, as required, of one of the following oils, all of which are recommended by B.S.A. Motor Cycles Ltd. and are suitable for summer and winter use: Shell Spirax 90EP; Mobil Mobilube GX90; Castrol Hypoy 90EP; B.P. Energol Gear oil 90EP; Texaco Multi-gear 90EP; or Esso Gear oil 90EP.

To top-up the gearbox to the correct level, first remove the oil-level screw from the centre of the drain plug, and also the gearbox oil-filler cap (*see* Figs. 10, 25). Then carefully pour some recommended oil through the oil-filler cap hole until surplus oil commences to drip from the hole from which

CORRECT LUBRICATION

the oil-level screw was removed. During this replenishment it is essential that the motor-cycle rests *on its wheels* on *level* ground. After completing replenishment, firmly tighten the oil-level screw; do this as soon as surplus oil ceases to drip away and make quite sure that the screw's fibre washer is in perfect condition; if in any doubt fit a new washer. No leakage must occur.

Drain and Refill Gearbox Every 5,000 *Miles.* On a *new* machine the oil should also be changed after covering the first 500 miles. Draining should preferably be done after finishing a ride. The oil in the unit-construction

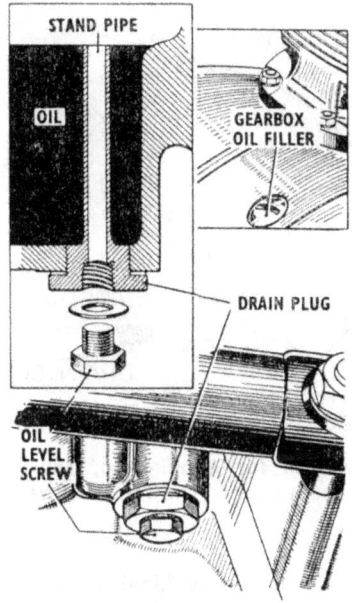

Fig 25 Showing provision for correctly replenishing and changing the gearbox oil

On 1968-9 models, the stand-pipe is superseded by a dip-stick attached to the filler-cap.

gearbox/crankcase is then warm and flows readily. Remove the drain plug and oil-level screw as a unit (applying a spanner to the *larger* hexagon) and allow all oil to drain off into a suitable receptacle.

Before replacing the drain plug/oil-level screw as a unit, check the condition of the rubber "O" ring or fibre washer (used on earlier models); if not perfect, renew it. Refill the gearbox with about $\frac{7}{8}$ pint of one of the previously recommended oils. To ensure that the oil level in the gearbox *is* correct, remove the oil-level screw (*see* Fig. 25) and use the method previously described for replenishing the gearbox every 2,000 miles. A dipstick attached to the filler-cap supersedes the stand-pipe for 1968–9 models.

Where Lubrication with Grease is Required. A number of items (wheel bearings, and various grease nipples) require the application of grease instead of oil at regular intervals. The following greases are recommended by B.S.A. Motor Cycles Ltd. for all 1962–9 A50 and A65 type models: Castrol Castrolease LM; Mobil Mobilgrease MP; Shell Retinax A; Esso Multi-purpose Grease H; B.P. Energrease L2; and Texaco Marfak Multi-purpose 2.

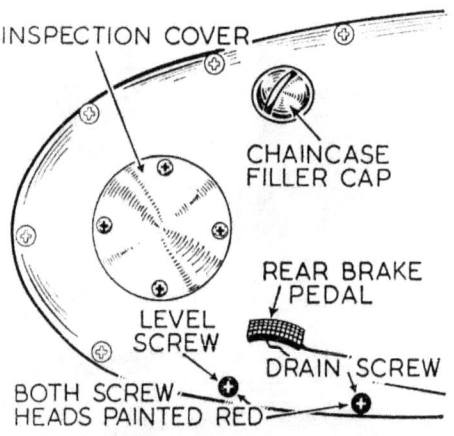

Fig 26   Showing provision for topping-up, and refilling, the primary chain case to the correct level

Lubricating Primary Chain. Every 2,000 miles check the oil level in the oil bath of the primary chaincase, made integral with the near side of the power unit. As in the case of the unit-construction gearbox, the oil bath (responsible also for lubricating the secondary chain and clutch) is quite independent of the engine as far as functioning is concerned. Its oil level normally falls very slowly.

For topping-up or refilling the oil-bath chaincase B.S.A. Motor Cycles Ltd. recommend for summer and winter use one of the following oils: Castrol Castrolite; Mobil Super; Shell Super 101; B.P. Energol Visco-Static 10W/4D; Motor Oil 10W/40; or Texaco Havoline 10W/30.

To top-up the oil-bath, first remove the level-screw (the *front* one with red-painted head), followed by the chaincase filter-cap. Both are shown in Fig. 26. Then through the cap hole pour in as required one of the above-mentioned oils. When doing this the motor-cycle must be resting on *both*

CORRECT LUBRICATION 53

wheels on a *level surface*. Allow all surplus oil to drain off into a suitable receptacle from the hole for the level-plug screw. Replace the filler-cap and level-screw, which must be firmly tightened.

Every 5,000 miles drain and refill the oil-bath which has a capacity of ¼ pint. Remove the drain screw (the rear one with red-painted head) shown in Fig. 26 and allow all oil to drain off, preferably after a run with the engine warm. Afterwards replace the drain screw and fill the oil-bath with about ¼ pint of one of the previously mentioned oils to the correct level as described in the preceding paragraph. When replacing the level and drain screws, especially the latter, make dead sure that they are firmly tightened to prevent any possible oil leakage.

Note that insufficient oil in the oil-bath causes unnecessary wear of the primary chain and sprocket teeth; excessive oil is very likely to result in some clutch-slip occurring. Never top-up or refill the oil-bath chaincase with any lubricant containing molybdenum disulphide or graphite, because these items may over-lubricate the clutch.

The Secondary Chain. Oil thrown off the primary chain collects in a small well at the rear of the primary chaincase from which a drip-feed automatically supplies a metered quantity of oil to the secondary chain. This oil supply is necessarily dependent on your maintaining suitable oil at the correct level in the primary chaincase.

In certain circumstances it is desirable to supplement the automatic drip-feed by applying an oil-can to the secondary chain while slowly rotating the rear wheel. The chain should always be kept moist with oil, and never dry.

To obtain the maximum useful life from a secondary chain it is advisable every 2,000–3,000 miles to remove it completely, wash it thoroughly in paraffin to remove all dirt and oil, hang it up to dry and then immerse it in a tray consisting of warm graphited grease or alternatively a mixture of warm melted tallow and powdered graphite. After allowing all surplus grease to drain off by hanging up the chain, replace the latter. When doing this it is imperative to check that the spring clip securing the connecting link has its *closed* end facing the direction of chain movement. On the top chain-run it should, of course, face *forward*.

The Steering Head Bearings. These are thoroughly packed with grease during their initial assembly and require subsequent repacking with grease at intervals of about 12,000 miles, when the bearing balls, cups and cones should be dismantled for careful inspection and renewal, if appreciable pitting and corrosion of the balls and/or pocketing and cracking of the cups and cones exists.

The Steering Lock. Do not insert oil into the key-hole of the built-in steering lock (*see* Fig. 4), as this may clog up the internal wards and wash away the special lubricant inserted before initial assembly. After completing a substantial mileage, however, it is permissible to apply a few drops of *thin machine oil* to the periphery of the moving drum.

Drain and Refill Front Forks Every 12,000 *Miles.* Alternatively, if your annual mileage is less than 12,000, change the damping oil once a year. Excessive movement of the telescopic fork legs generally indicates that

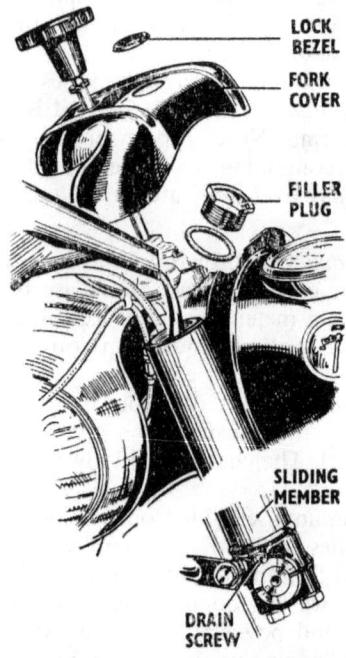

Fig 27 Refilling B.S.A. front fork legs on a B.S.A. Twin with headlamp mounted in a fork cover

The general procedure for draining and filling the telescopic front forks is the same on all 1962-9 A50 and A65 type models irrespective of the headlamp mounting.

draining and renewal of the oil *has* become necessary. Occasionally, however, failure of the oil seals mid-way up the fork legs causes oil leakage and the same symptoms.

On B.S.A. twins having the Lucas headlamp mounted in a fork cover (e.g. on many "Star" models) it is necessary before draining the damping oil first to remove the steering-head lock bezel (*see* Fig. 27) and also the steering-damper knob and attached rod. Then take off the fork cover.

Where no fork cover is provided, as shown in Fig. 3, these instructions do not, of course, apply.

To drain the telescopic front forks, remove the two filler plugs and drain screws from the lower ends of the fork sliding members (*see* Fig. 27) and allow all the damping oil possible to drain off into suitable receptacles. After several minutes of draining, apply the front brake and "pump" the forks up and down to expel any oil remaining inside the fork legs. If preferred, each fork leg can be dealt with separately.

To refill the front forks with S.A.E. 20 damping oil, replace and firmly tighten the two drain screws, making sure that their fibre washers are replaced and in sound condition. Then pour into each fork leg, as shown in Fig. 27, ⅓ pint of one of the oils recommended on page 52 for the primary chaincase. Finally replace and very firmly tighten the two filler plugs, not omitting to fit their washers.

The Rear Suspension. The telescopic hydraulic-damper units with totally enclosed coil springs are sealed during manufacture and no subsequent replenishment of the hydraulic fluid is necessary or possible. Should the damper units become inefficient, there is no remedy but to renew the units.

The "swinging arm" pivots have bonded rubber or "Silentbloc" bushes and these do not require any lubrication.

Front and Rear Hubs. All 1962 and later B.S.A. twins have full-width hubs with ball-journal bearings which are packed with grease during assembly; this grease should suffice for about 12,000 miles or until a complete overhaul is necessary; the bearings should then be dismantled, thoroughly cleaned and repacked with grease.

Where a sidecar is attached, lubricate the bearings of its wheel and also its chassis in accordance with the maker's instructions.

Front and Rear Brakes. Every 2,000 miles inject some grease (one shot with the grease-gun) through the two grease nipples provided for the brake cam spindles on the front and rear wheels of 1962–4 models. On 1965–8 models only the cam spindle for the front wheel has a grease nipple. On the 1968 "Lightning" and "Spitfire" models with 8 in. diameter twin leading-shoe front brakes and all 1969 models, *two* grease nipples are provided (*see* Fig. 28) and the linkage pins must also be attended to. Be most careful not to inject excessive grease, otherwise some of it may reach the brake-shoe linings and badly impair braking efficiency.

Where no grease nipple is provided for the rear-brake cam spindle, lubrication should be effected by applying 2–3 drops of oil to the cam spindle through the hole exposed by turning the spring clip.

Also every 2,000 miles grease the pivot for the rear-brake pedal and the brake-rod pivot pin. Where a transverse brake cross-shaft is provided (many 1962–5 models) about every 2,000 miles remove and regrease the shaft (*see* Fig. 29) as described below.

Slacken off the rear brake adjustment (*see* page 113) to remove any tension in the cable or (on 1963–9 models) brake rod; then mark the off-side end of the shaft and its operating lever so that it is possible to replace the latter on the same serrations (essential to ensure good braking action). Next remove the pinch-bolt from the operating lever: tap the shaft through the

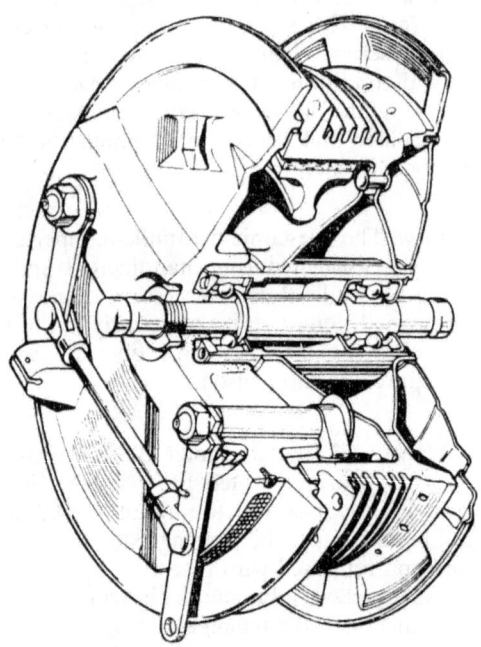

Fig 28   On 1968–9 Models with twin leading-shoe front brakes do not forget to apply the grease-gun every 2,000 miles to the two cam-spindle nipples and also to oil the linkage pins

lever and withdraw the shaft, complete with the rear-brake pedal from the near side of the motor-cycle. Wipe the shaft clean, smear some new grease on it and finally reassemble in the reverse order of dismantling.

Where a Cable-operated Rear Brake is Provided. The cable return spring and threaded sleeve are enclosed by a rubber protector and the cable can be released by completely unscrewing the adjuster. Occasionally (about ever 2,000 miles) grease the cable, its threaded sleeve and return spring. Afterwards reposition the rubber protector and screw up the adjuster as required.

CORRECT LUBRICATION 57

Control Levers, Exposed Cables and Linkage. To prevent corrosion, and to maintain smooth action, it is advisable occasionally (say, every 2,000 miles) to apply a few drops of engine oil (*see* page 42) to these items with an oil-can. Besides oiling the handlebar control levers, apply some oil to all external brake linkage. Note that the throttle twist-grip itself requires no lubrication.

Where exposed portions of control cables are concerned, grease (*see* page 52) is a preferable alternative. Note that on all 1966 and later B.S.A. twins the control cable inner wires on new machines are treated throughout their length with molybdenum-based grease a semi-permanent form of

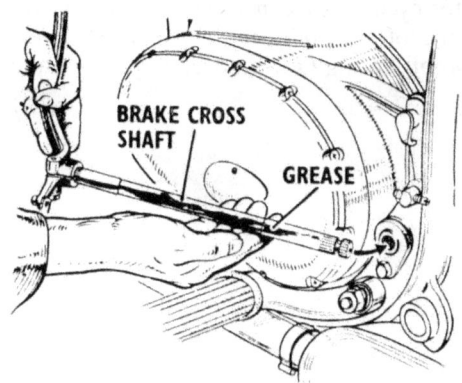

Fig 29   Greasing rear-brake cross-shaft
Applicable to 1962–5 "Star" models and the 1964–5 A65R "Rocket."

lubrication requiring little further attention. A grease nipple is fitted to the clutch cable on 1969 models and the cable should be thoroughly greased every 2,000 miles. Keep all control cables quite clear of the upper portion of the engine, otherwise the lubricant in the cable casings will gradually dry up.

It is desirable to grease (not oil) speedometer driving-cables, but the application of excessive grease must always be avoided, otherwise some of it may enter the head of the Smith's instrument. On B.S.A. twins with exposed speedometer heads it is only necessary to unscrew the cable nipple below the head and then pull out the inner wire for thorough cleaning and greasing. Grease should be applied sparingly and not further than within six inches of the speedometer head.

An excellent long-term and reliable method of oiling a control cable connected to one of the handlebar levers is to disconnect the Bowden cable connection from the handlebar lever, and with some brown paper devise a suitable funnel; attach this to the cable casing, using a rubber band to secure it. Then pour some engine oil into the funnel and allow this to trickle slowly down between the casing and cable.

The Dipper Switch. Lubricate every 5,000 miles the moving parts of the dipper switch (*see* Fig. 4) with a little *thin* oil. Apply one drop only, otherwise you may start a short-circuit.

Grease Central Stand Pivot. This should be done every 2,000 miles and two grease nipples are provided for grease-gun application.

Easing Rusted Parts. Rusted items, such as bolts or nuts, on the power unit or the motor-cycle itself can usually be satisfactorily eased by the application of one of the following six oils: Shell Donax P; Castrol; B.P. Energol; Mobil Spring Oil; Esso or Regent Graphited "Penetrating Oil."

4 Lucas A.C./D.C. Lighting and Ignition

Brief Outline of System. The "heart" of the combined Lucas lighting and ignition system is an alternator (Fig. 30) having its rotor (the sole moving part) driven by an extension of the crankshaft. The alternating current (a.c.) supplied by the alternator is converted into uni-directional current (d.c.) by a rectifier and it then charges the battery (two batteries on most 1966-7 B.S.A. twins). The alternator output in all three lighting-switch

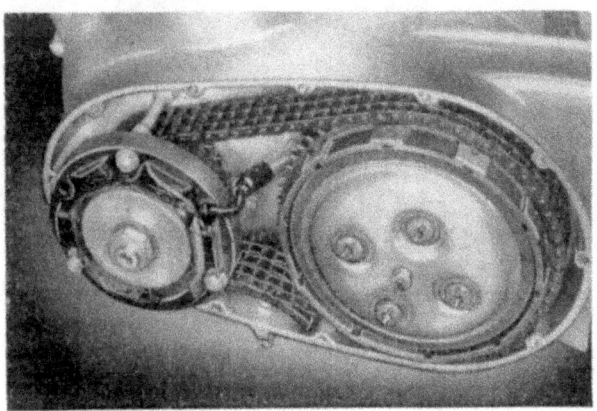

Fig 30 Oil-bath chaincase with cover removed showing Lucas alternator and its three output cables

Note also (at the rear) the B.S.A. clutch driven from the crankshaft sprocket by a triple row chain with tensioning slipper adjustable from outside the chaincase.

positions (*see* page 12) is automatically controlled according to the state of battery charge.

From the battery, or batteries, current is taken direct for lighting and via a contact-breaker (driven from the timing idler gear) and two ignition coils (one for each cylinder) to spark the two ignition plugs. On some pre-1966 models it is possible to start up the engine even if the battery is badly discharged, the ignition switch having an "EMG" position (*see* page 8). How to obtain and maintain maximum illumination from your lamps, and non-stop "fat" sparks from your plugs will now be considered.

MAINTENANCE REQUIRED

The Alternator. On 1962–7 B.S.A. A50 and A65 type twins a Lucas model RM19 (RM21 for 1968–9) alternator is specified. This comprises a 6-coil laminated stator spigot-mounted in the primary chaincase ahead of the clutch, as shown in Fig. 30, with a hexagonal steel core, each face of which carries a high-energy permanent magnet keyed to a laminated pole-tip.

On all B.S.A. models the alternator for 6-v circuits is designed for use

Fig 31   Frame compartment (with cover removed) housing Lucas battery and rectifier

This applies to 1962–5 B.S.A. twins provided with a single 6-volt battery without a zener diode to control battery charging. The rectifier, as may be seen, is mounted on a bracket at the top right-hand corner of the battery.

with headlamp bulbs not exceeding 30/24 watts rating and 50/40 watts for 12-v systems. The stator and rotor can, should necessity arise, be separated without its being necessary to fit magnetic keepers to the rotor poles.

As regards alternator maintenance, all that is required is to make quite sure that the three snap connectors for the output cables (coloured green) are kept *clean and tight*.

The Rectifier. This is mounted on a bracket on the near side of the motorcycle behind the right-hand top corner of the battery as shown in Fig. 31, The Lucas type 2DS506 (FSX 1849 for 1962–3) rectifier comprises four

LUCAS A.C./D.C. LIGHTING AND IGNITION

plates (covered on one side with selenium) and functions as a non-return valve, permitting current to pass in *one direction* only; it thereby converts alternating current (a.c.) from the alternator into unidirectional current (d.c.) for battery charging.

The rectifier requires no maintenance beyond occasionally checking that its three connections are clean and tight and that the nut provided to secure this semi-conductor device to its mounting bracket on the motor-cycle frame is *always* kept firmly tightened. When tightening the nut securing the rectifier, hold the bolt head with another spanner as indicated in Fig. 32. Note that the securing nut and bolt both have ¼ in. × 28 U.N.F. threads, and circles are marked on them to indicate this.

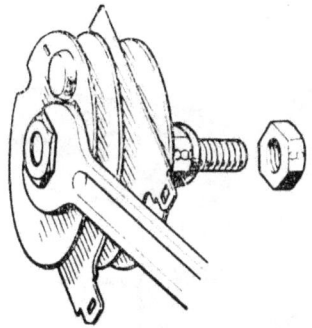

Fig 32 When tightening the nut securing the rectifier unit to its mounting bracket, always hold the bolt head with another spanner

(B.S.A. Workshop Manual)

In *no circumstances* ever slacken the two nuts which actually clamp the rectifier plates together. Their degree of tightening is most carefully decided during initial assembly, and any subsequent alteration is very likely to affect adversely the functioning of the rectifier unit.

A zener-diode was fitted to 1967–9 models to control the charging rate to the battery. It must always have 100 per cent contact with its seating face (i.e. perfectly flat and square) and must be tightened with a torque of 17 lb in.

Topping-up Battery Cells. On all 1962–5 B.S.A. twins a Lucas MLZ9E 6-volt battery is mounted adjacent to the rectifier as shown in Fig. 31. The 1966 and subsequent B.S.A. models have 12-volt battery equipment which includes two Lucas MKZ9E 6-volt batteries (*see* Fig. 33) connected in series to give 12 volts, or on most later models a single Lucas PUZ5A 12-volt battery (*see* Fig. 34), connected in series with a zener diode in circuit to control battery charging.

All Lucas MLZ9E, MKZ9E and PUZ5A batteries have moulded cases in translucent polystyrene to enable the level of the electrolyte to be visible from *outside* the battery.

At weekly intervals, or about every 250 miles (more frequently in hot climates), carefully check the level of the electrolyte in each cell and top-up as required with *distilled* water. Never use tap water. Lift the battery from its carrier so that the *electrolyte level* (indicated by a coloured line) is clearly visible. Then remove the battery cover, unscrew the filler plugs and with a syringe top up each cell with distilled water until the electrolyte level is up to the coloured line. On no account top up to the level of the separator guard.

Do not add distilled water while the battery is on charge (on or removed from the motor-cycle) and *in no circumstances* hold a naked flame close

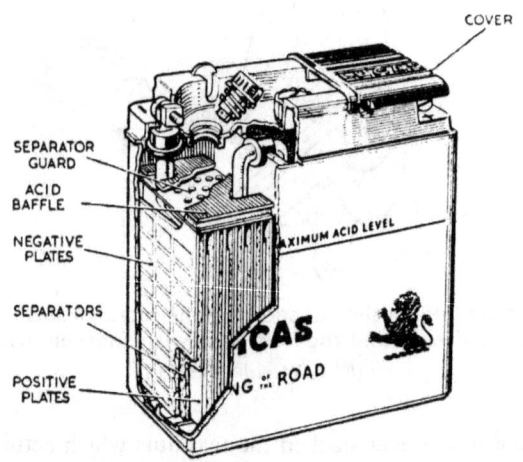

Fig 33 Cut-away view showing details of Lucas 6-volt MLZ9E or MKZ9E battery

to a vent-hole, otherwise gas composed of oxygen and hydrogen may cause an explosion to the detriment of you and your battery!

Other Essential Battery Maintenance. About every 1,000 miles, or monthly, and more frequently in hot climates, remove the battery cover and thoroughly clean it. Also closely inspect the battery connections which must be kept clean and tight. Scrape off all corrosion present on the terminals, and afterwards lightly smear them with some petroleum jelly. Before replacing the vent plugs, check that all vent-holes are unobstructed and that the rubber washer provided for each vent-plug is in perfect condition; if not renew it.

LUCAS A.C./D.C. LIGHTING AND IGNITION 63

Never leave your battery badly discharged. Should your B.S.A. be out of commission for some reason for a considerable time, get its battery or batteries fully charged and then every fortnight have it or them given a short refreshing charge. This will eliminate the risk of the battery plates becoming permanently sulphated.

The correct specific gravity (S.G.) *of the electrolyte*, with the battery fully charged (in the U.K.), is 1·270–1·290 for each cell. For checking the

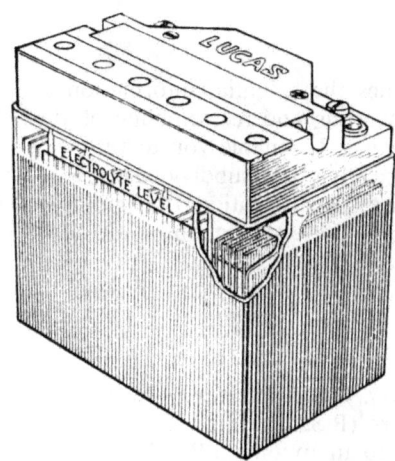

Fig 34 Cut-away view of Lucas 12-volt PUZ5A battery

S.G. (rarely necessary) of batteries fitted to 1962–9 B.S.A. twins, the use of a *miniature* hydrometer is necessary.

There is not sufficient space in this handbook to include wiring diagrams for the complete range of models. Provided that your electrical equipment is properly maintained (e.g. the prevention of chafing of the cables against the frame, etc.) it is unlikely that you will need such a diagram. However, wiring diagrams are included in all B.S.A. Workshop Manuals and, in most cases, separate diagrams can be obtained from the Service Dept. of Messrs. Joseph Lucas in Birmingham. It will be of great assistance to them if you quote not only the name of your model but the year of manufacture.

5 General Maintenance

This chapter includes the essential information concerning the routine maintenance, dismantling and reassembling of 1962-9 B.S.A. type A50 and A65 vertical twins. To enable you to turn quickly to the particular instructions you need it has been subdivided into a number of main sections. All detailed references to carburation, the lighting system, and lubrication have been omitted, as these subjects have already been comprehensively dealt with in Chapters 2 to 4.

Attend to maintenance regularly and conscientiously, and do not wait until your mount "calls out" for attention.

Spares and Repairs. When you have occasion to forward or deliver any parts to the makers (B.S.A. Motor Cycles Ltd., Service Department, Birmingham 11) or to an appointed B.S.A. dealer, do not forget to attach to each part a label bearing clearly your *full name and address*. To facilitate identification of a part or unit, always quote the year of manufacture and the model (e.g. 1967 A65 Thunderbolt) also the engine and frame numbers (*see* page 5).

Note that useful illustrated spare-parts lists are obtainable from appointed spares stockists who are widely distributed throughout the United Kingdom and maintain a comprehensive stock of B.S.A. spares; some of them undertake general servicing and repair work.

Items Needed for Maintenance. You must have handy in your garage or workshop other tools in addition to the standard tool kit. These items include: a can of paraffin and a stiff brush for cleaning components; tins of suitable oils for the engine and gearbox; a small funnel for topping up the gearbox or oil tank; a canister of grease and a grease-gun: a large drip tray; a medium-sized bowl or similar article for washing parts in paraffin; plenty of clean non-fluffy rags; a tin of valve-grinding paste (coarse and fine); and a set of engine gaskets.

You should also have available: a set of new gudgeon pin circlips; a pair of medium-size cutting pliers; a small electrical screwdriver; and a valve spring compressor (*see* page 82). A gudgeon-pin extractor may also prove useful. It is desirable to obtain a set of feeler gauges for checking

GENERAL MAINTENANCE 65

tappet clearances plug gap, etc., and also a sparking plug re-gapping tool (*see* page 68).

For good maintenance of the motor-cycle parts you should obtain: a tyre pressure gauge; a box of spare chain links; a chain rivet extractor; a couple of sponges and a pail (if a hose is not available) for washing down; a good wax polish for the enamelled parts; and last, but by no means least, a good hand-cleanser, e.g. "Swarfega" or similar preparation.

Tools for Repair Work. It is obviously desirable to rig up a suitable bench, complete with vice, and to purchase some extra tools. These need not be many in number and could comprise a mallet: medium-weight hammer: a small hand drill (and twist drills): a hacksaw: a selection of files: and a soldering outfit. General repair work is beyond the scope of this book, because appreciable technical knowledge is required and not a little skill in the handling of tools.

Should you wish to undertake re-bushing of any components, this will require the use of appropriate extractors, punches, etc., a job preferably dealt with by authorized B.S.A. repairers. Special B.S.A. service tools are obtainable through any B.S.A. spares stockist.

Cleaning the Motor-cycle. If you develop the bad habit of allowing your machine to remain dirty, defects may pass unobserved, rusting will certainly occur, performance may decline to some extent and, of course, depreciation will inevitably be more rapid than it should be. If possible do not leave your machine soaking wet overnight.

Cleaning the Engine/Gearbox Unit. Keep the cylinder barrel fins clean and black (not the cylinder head fins, these are of aluminium). If the fins are bare, coat them with some proprietary cylinder black after thorough cleaning with a stiff brush dipped in paraffin. In addition to spoiling the appearance of the engine, rusty fins also reduce good dispersion of heat. Scour the lower part of the engine and gearbox with stiff brushes and paraffin and dry off with clean rag. As an alternative for very dirty engines, paint the surfaces with a special cleaning compound such as "Gunk" and then wash off. Use a rag damped in paraffin for cleaning bright parts. Stripped-down components should also be thoroughly cleaned in paraffin and spread out on a clean sheet of paper.

Cleaning Enamelled Parts. Never remove dry and caked mud from enamelled parts because this will damage the surfaces. Use a hose to soak the mud off or copious supplies of water from a large sponge. If a hose is used, avoid spraying direct on to the carburettor, hubs, etc. Tar spots may be removed with turpentine. Dry the enamelled parts with a good chamois leather, polish with soft dusters and finish with a good polish such as "Autobrite." Riders who seldom use their machine in bad weather can keep it in good condition by rubbing the enamel over with a paraffin-damped rag, followed by a dry duster.

Cleaning the Chromium Plating. Do not use liquid metal polish or paste. Use a proprietary cleaning compound if you must, but it is better to remove all forms of tarnish with a damp chamois leather and restore the finish with a soft duster.

Tightness of Nuts. During the running-in period check the tightness of the various nuts. Some of these are self-locking, but all the remainder require checking because some initial bedding down of components usually occurs. Pay particular attention to drain plugs, pipe unions and the like.

After about the first 250 miles from new (and also following reassembly after decarbonizing) check the tightness of the cylinder head bolts. If attention is required, possibly due to settling down of the cylinder head gasket, tighten the bolts a little at a time, "criss-crossing" the head from one bolt to the next. The centre bolt cannot be tightened until the push rods are removed and the exhaust rocker and spindle must be dismantled to give access to the front two bolts. Following completion of running-in, it will be sufficient if the various nuts and bolts are checked for tightness about once a month.

Adjustment and Maintenance of the Carburettor. This is dealt with in detail in Chapter 2.

Lubrication Instructions. Comprehensive instructions concerning the lubrication of the 1962–9 A50 and A65 models are given in Chapter 3 and the lubrication chart (Fig. 24) summarizes the lubrication requirements.

CARE OF THE IGNITION SYSTEM

All models described in this handbook are fitted with a Lucas alternator mounted on the driving side of the crankshaft. Similarly, automatic ignition advance and retard mechanism is fitted throughout the range. The majority of models utilize a battery and coil ignition (with a detachable ignition key) but a few of the purely sporting models have "energy-transfer" ignition and require a cut-out button to stop the engine (*see* page 8).

Recommended Sparking Plugs. To ensure easy starting, a cool-running engine, and maximum performance throughout the throttle range, it is essential always to run on a suitable type of sparking plug. All B.S.A. twins run on 14 mm size plugs. The makers recommend Champion sparking plugs. For machines used in the United Kingdom, suppressors must

GENERAL MAINTENANCE

be fitted by law to avoid interference with television sets. The suppressors are usually added to the high-tension cable adjacent to the plug, or built-in with the plug cover. Later models (from about 1967) have h.t. cables which themselves act as suppressors and hence no separate suppressor is fitted. These cables can be identified by a greenish appearance.

For regular bad-weather riding, it is as well to fit a water-proof terminal cover which will suit any of the Champion plugs detailed in the following table and also accommodate a suppressor.

Only two Champion sparking plugs are recommended by the manufacturers for the whole range of B.S.A. twins made between 1962 and 1965 inclusive. The first of these is the N4, which was used in all models up to 1966. Thereafter, this plug was used on single carburettor models only, the two-carburettor high-performance engines being fitted with the colder type N3 plug. Alternative brands are shown in the table below.

SPARKING PLUG RECOMMENDATIONS FOR ALL A50 AND A65 ENGINES

B.S.A. Model	Champion	Lodge	KLG	NGK
All models 1962–5	N4	HLN	FE75	B-8E
Single carburettor engines, 1966–9	N4	HLN	FE75	B-8E
Two carburettor engines, 1966–9	N3	2HLN	FE80	B-9E

The Plug Points Gap. A recommended type of sparking plug remains serviceable for many thousands of miles, but in due course the electrodes gradually burn away until the gap between them becomes excessive, causing difficult starting and occasional misfiring at low speeds. Check the points gap at intervals of about 2,000 miles and re-set the gap if necessary. The correct gap is between 0·020 in. and 0·025 in.

To check the gap, use a feeler gauge of the appropriate thickness, or a gauge attached to a Champion plug gap tool (*see* Fig. 35). The feeler should just slide between the centre and outer (or earth) electrodes. Note the thickness of the gauge and if adjustment is necessary, bend the *earth electrode only* towards the centre electrode, using the slotted blade attached to the gapping tool. *Never attempt to bend the centre electrode*, because this may damage the insulation, in which case the plug becomes unusable.

Sparking plugs should be replaced every 10,000 miles.

Cleaning a Sparking Plug. Provided that excessive oil is not entering the combustion chamber (indicated by *blue* smoke from the exhaust) and that the carburettor is correctly adjusted (a rich mixture gives *black* smoke from the exhaust), the plug points should remain serviceable until scheduled for cleaning. The base of the body should be smooth and black, with the centre insulation retaining its natural colour. Excessive oil causes a heavy black carbon deposit and gumminess, a weak mixture causes the end of the plug to whiten and a rich mixture causes a deposit of dry soot. Hence, to the knowledgeable eye, the state of the sparking plug can give a good idea of the condition of the engine. Cleaning of the plugs and checking the points gap should be carried out at the same time.

Quick cleaning of the plugs can be done by brushing the points and slightly rubbing their firing sides with smooth emery cloth. Thorough cleaning, and this specially involves internal cleaning, requires the services of garage equipment.

All the plugs quoted in the table on page 67 are of the non-detachable type (i.e. they cannot be dismantled for cleaning) and consequently must be cleaned on "air-blast" equipment kept by most garages. Within a very

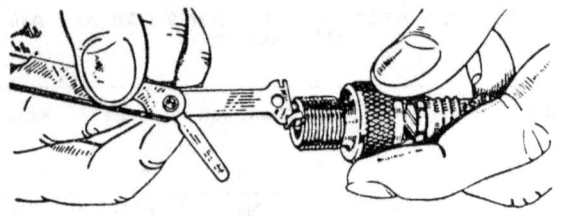

Fig 35 Using a Champion sparking plug gapping tool

Feeler gauges of varying sizes are contained in both ends of the holder and the tool also carries a fine file for trimming the electrodes.

short time each plug, subjected to a jet of compressed air containing an abrasive compound, is cleaned both internally and externally. It is then tested for sparking under pressure (to simulate the conditions in the cylinder), when a faulty plug can be detected immediately. The only cure for this is to replace it with a new one in accordance with the details given in the table. If the plug sparks satisfactorily, trim the points with a fine file in order to restore flat, parallel faces and re-set the gap to 0·020 in.–0·025 in.

Fitting the Plug. Modern Champion plugs are supplied complete with a non-detachable steel washer, specially designed to last for the life of the plug. Do not try to remove the washer. Make sure that the threads in the cylinder head are clean in addition to those on the plug. Screw the plug home as far as possible *by hand* and use a box spanner for the final tightening. Never use an adjustable spanner for this purpose.

The Contact-breaker. Lubrication of the cam bearing, felt-pad, etc., is dealt with on page 48. The contact-breaker, complete with its automatic

GENERAL MAINTENANCE

ignition advance-and-retard mechanism, is housed in the timing case on the right side of the crankcase and is accessible after removing the circular inspection cover.

Examine the contact points (Figs. 36 and 37). There are two sets of these, one set for each cylinder and on models from 1962–7 the backplate also carries the capacitors. In later years, the capacitors are mounted elsewhere on the machine. If the contact faces are blackened or pitted, clean them with a fine carborundum stone, taking care to keep the faces parallel with each

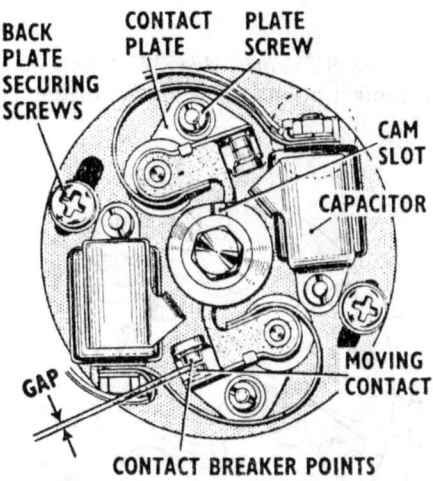

Fig 36 The Lucas contact-breaker assembly for all 1962–7 Models

Note the correct position of the cam slot for applying one spot of lubricating oil (see page 48). A small oil-moistened felt pad is carried in the capacitor bracket to maintain a film of lubricant on the cam surface.

other and also restore the slightly convex surfaces. If the pitting is deep it will be as well to replace the complete contact-breaker assembly.

Checking the Gaps. First remove the sparking plugs, which will allow the starter pedal to be pushed down by hand and so enable the engine to be rotated without undue resistance. Turn the engine slowly until the highest point of the cam (at the centre of the contact-breaker) has moved round and separated one pair of contact points. (Only one contact moves, the ot ıer is stationary.) At this position the gap should be 0·015 in., a figure which should be verified with feeler gauges. This check needs to be carried out every 2,000 miles (and also after the first 500 miles from new). Repeat this procedure for the second pair of contact points. Any appreciable variation from the recommended gap should be rectified as detailed below.

Gap Adjustment (1962–7 *Engines*), *Fig.* 36. The stationary contact point is attached to a small plate and for any adjustment to be made, its retaining screw must be slackened. The plate can then be moved by a small amount either way, until the gap between the contact points is correct. Re-tighten the retaining screw and check the gap again. A slight modification to the contact plate for 1966–7 models introduced a slot into this plate and two small inverted dimples in theback plate (which carries the whole of the contact-breaker units and capacitors). These features enable a small screwdriver to be used for "levering" the contact base plate into a new position.

Gap Adjustment (1968–9 *Engines*), *Fig.* 37. A new design with simplified adjustment of the contact points gap and also of the ignition setting, was

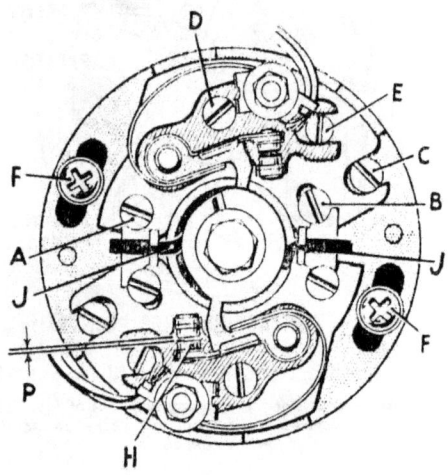

Fig 37   The Lucas contact-breaker assembly for all 1968–9 Models

In the case of the 1969 models only, the cam bearing is treated with a dry lubricant by the manufacturers and further lubrication is unnecessary. This type of contact-breaker carries two felt pads J, for the 1968 models.

used on all B.S.A. twins from 1968 onwards. The alterations involved more space requirements than previously, and for this reason the capacitors were no longer mounted on the back plate, but in a self-contained unit elsewhere on the machine. Check the fully open gap in the manner already described and if adjustment is necessary slacken (but do not remove) screw *D* and rotate the eccentric pin *E* until the gap is correct. Turning the pin *E* has the effect of moving the plate which carries the stationary contact point and hence of varying the gap between the contact points. Tighten the screw *D* firmly and check the gap again.

IGNITION TIMING

The importance of accurate ignition timing cannot be over-emphasized, but no attempt should be made to "improve" on the figure given below. The makers have evolved the correct ignition setting after much development work and more harm than good will result from changing to a different ignition setting.

All B.S.A. twins have gear-driven contact-breakers and the operating cam is mounted on a tapered shaft; for these reasons it is most unlikely that the original ignition timing will have altered. The exception to this is that if the contact-breaker gap varies from the recommended figure a change in timing also occurs (a wider gap gives advanced timing and a smaller gap retards the timing). It follows that if the ignition timing is being checked or re-set, *the contact-breaker points should be examined first*, and the gap between them corrected if necessary.

To set the ignition timing requires patience, but is not beyond the capabilities of an amateur mechanic. All coil ignition B.S.A. twins, whether 500 c.c. or 650 c.c., should be timed at 34° before top dead centre (T.D.C.), fully advanced, i.e. the spark must occur when the crankshaft is at 34° before its highest position in the direction of rotation or, in other words, before the piston is at the top of its stroke. For models with energy-transfer ignition, the timings are 500 c.c.–23° before T.D.C. and 650 c.c.–28° before T.D.C. Formerly, B.S.A. advised setting the ignition timing by using piston distances before T.D.C. and with the ignition fully retarded, but since the dimensions were so small they were difficult to measure and preference is now given to timing the ignition in degrees and at full advance. Also the manufacturing tolerances on the auto-mechanism causes a slight variation in the range between maximum advance and maximum retard and hence, in the interests of accurate timing, since the advanced position is the most important, any small variation in timing is preferable at the retarded position.

The mechanism is located behind the contact-breaker backplate and if you grasp the cam at the centre of the unit you will see that, if it is turned in one direction and then released, it flies back to its original position. This is at full retard and for timing the ignition the cam, which is attached to the mechanism, must be set in the advanced position. To do this, remove the bolt which retains the cam, remove its washer and substitute another having a larger hole. Replace the bolt, rotate the cam to its limit in an anti-clockwise direction, hold in position, and tighten the bolt. The new washer will lock against the cam side face and prevent its return to the retard position.

Determining the Piston Position (1962–4 *Engines*). Before checking the timing, obtain a degree plate. These are sometimes given away as advertising material, but it is a simple matter to make such a plate of stout card. It should be about 6 in. diameter and be marked out in degrees at the rim.

Remove the primary chaincase cover, mount the degree plate centrally on the mainshaft in approximately the T.D.C. position, and add a pointer to some convenient stud. Select the right-side piston which must be at the top of its stroke with both its valves closed (compression stroke). T.D.C. can then be determined accurately if some form of abutment is made to limit the piston travel, e.g. it can take the form of an extension to an old sparking plug (but make sure it does not foul one of the valves). Still working with the right-side piston, bring it gently against its abutment by turning the engine as far as it will go forwards and then backwards. (The engine can be rotated backwards if top gear is engaged and the rear wheel

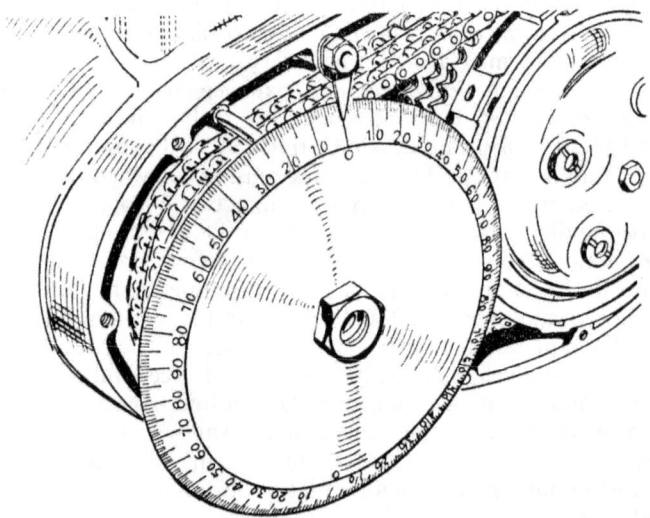

Fig 38 Setting the ignition timing with the aid of a degree plate

In the position shown, the pistons are at T.D.C. and the plate has been readjusted until the zero mark and the pointer coincide. This operation is greatly simplified if it is made when the cylinder head has been taken off, e.g. when decarbonizing. It is a simple matter for the engine to be turned backwards by the required number of degrees.

turned carefully.) Degree plate readings can be taken in each position and the point midway between them will be an accurate top dead centre. Re-set the degree plate to the precise position (Fig. 38). It is now an easy matter to turn the engine backwards by exactly 34° and so setting the piston in the correct position for timing the ignition.

Determining the Piston Position (1965–8 *Engines*). The operation is much simplified on these engines and is effective from 1965 engine Nos. A65A-1625, A65C-1986, and A65DC3456, A65B-410, A65E-1149, A50B

GENERAL MAINTENANCE 73

and A50BC524, A50A-1271, A65Ap-330, A50D and A50DC-102, A50P-142. A special aperture is provided in the front of the right-side half of the crankcase and covered by a small plate *A* (Fig. 39). A round timing "plug" on which a flat surface is machined, is available as a B.S.A. Service Tool under Part No. 68-710, and its dimensions are such that it will just fit in a slot machined in the flywheel. Rotate the engine very slowly by hand until the right-side piston is rising on its compression stroke (when both valves can be inspected through the sparking plug aperture and seen to be closed). Insert the timing plug through the aperture and into the flywheel slot;

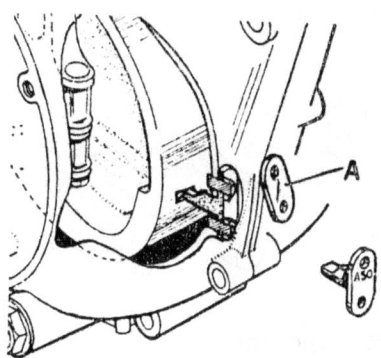

Fig 39 Using the timing plug, 1965–8 engines

This is shown both in and out of position to clarify the positions of the "flat" in relation to the flywheel. If inverted, an incorrect ignition timing will be given.

then add and tighten its fixing nuts. It is important to note that the timing plug must be fitted with the symbol A50 at the top (ignore symbol A65) and that this applies to both 500 c.c. and 650 c.c. engines. If the timing plug is not marked, fit it with the "cut-away" portion at the top. The right-side piston is now correctly placed for timing the ignition for this cylinder and when this is completed (*see* below), remove the timing plug, rotate the engine through one revolution and re-insert the plug. The left-side piston is then ready for timing.

Determining the Piston Position (1969 *Engines*). The method for these engines is similar to that for the 1965–8 models, except that the timing plug screws into the crankcase and its plunger *B* (Fig. 40) registers with a round hole in the flywheel. This tool is B.S.A. part No. 60-1859. The aperture is sealed by the plug *A*.

Timing the Ignition (1962–7 *Engines*). Since the right-side piston was the first to be set in its proper position for timing, the upper pair of contact points should be *just* opening if the timing is correct. If not, slacken the two backplate securing screws (Fig. 36) and move the plate round by a very small amount until the contact points comply with this condition. Firmly tighten the two screws.

When the left-side piston is in its correct timing position (*see* previous section) examine the lower pair of contact points. If any adjustment is

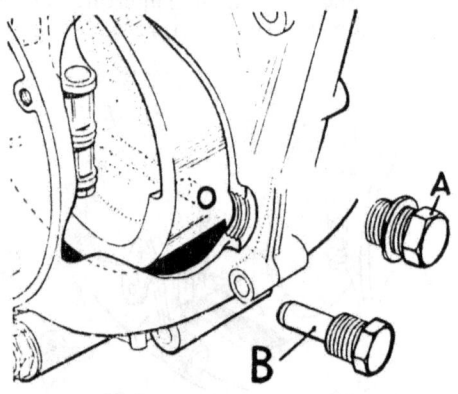

Fig 40   Using the timing plug, 1969 engines

This design obviates any possibility of error since the plunger B is cylindrical. On later versions of this tool the plunger is a sliding fit in the body, which allows its location in the flywheel to be felt more readily by the fingers.

required in this case, *do not alter the position of the backplate*, but readjust the contact points themselves until they meet the given requirement. Obviously, this will affect the fully open gap slightly but it is the only way in which very small manufacturing tolerances can be accommodated.

Timing the Ignition (1968–9 *Engines*). Redesign of the contact-breaker unit simplified still further the adjustment or re-setting of the ignition timing, by making the contact-breakers completely independent of each other and hence independently adjustable. All that is required if adjustment is necessary is to slacken screws *A* and *B* (Fig. 37) and gently rotate the eccentric pin *C* until the contact points are just separating. Firmly tighten *A* and *B*.

When the engine has been rotated and the left-side piston is in the correct position for ignition timing, repeat the procedure for this set of contact points.

Separation of the Contact-breaker Points. Previous paragraphs under "Ignition Timing" have referred to the fact that the contact points must

GENERAL MAINTENANCE   75

be *just* opening, and this precise instant is not always easy to detect by eye.
   One way of overcoming this problem is to connect a battery and bulb in series with the contact points (Fig. 41). Attach one lead from the "C"-spring to a battery terminal, another lead from the second battery terminal to the bulb and a third connection from the second pole of the bulb

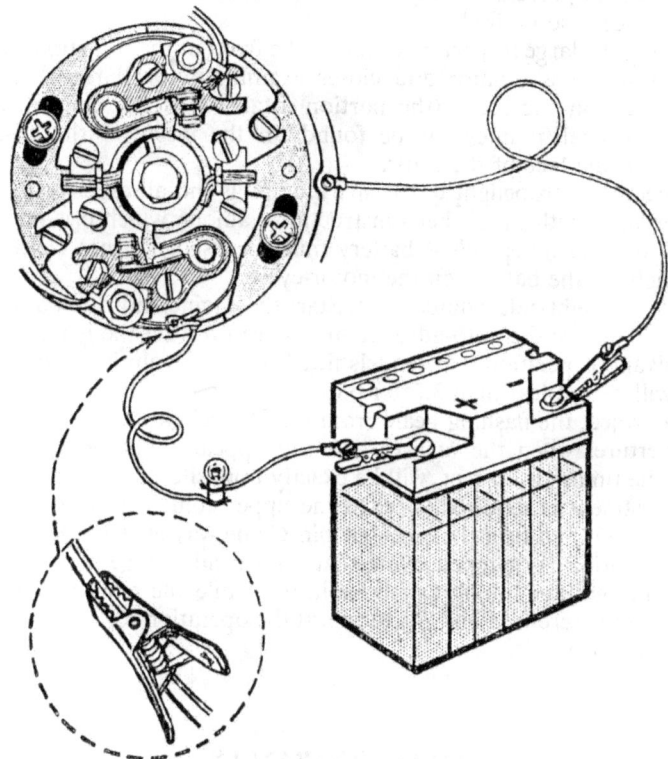

Fig 41   An electrical method for obtaining an accurate opening of the contact points

Pincer-type clips are the quickest way of making good electrical connections. The illustration shows the connections for the left cylinder and for the right cylinder the pincer clip must be attached to the upper contact-breaker spring.

to the engine. The light will be extinguished when the points begin to open and the circuit is broken. Change the lead to the second "C"-spring for checking the opening of the second pair of contact points.
   Alternatively, slip a piece of very thin paper (cigarette paper will do very well) between the contact points, which will be just opening when the paper can be withdrawn by a gentle pull.

Timing the Ignition by "Strobelight" (1967-9 Engines). The methods given earlier for timing the ignition can give excellent results, but in 1967 B.S.A. introduced an even more precise method of carrying out this operation, using a well-known scientific principle. This involves the use of a "Strobelight," an instrument specially designed for its purpose and which, when in action, has the effect of bringing rotating parts to a standstill. Many B.S.A. dealers possess this equipment, but it can also be purchased at a modest price if so desired.

Opening the large inspection cover on the front of the primary chaincase will expose the alternator and closer examination will reveal a radial line marked on the rotor (the portion attached to the crankshaft). In addition a small pointer will be found on the inside of the chaincase opposite to the face of the rotor.

Connect the Strobelight to the sparking plug and all other connections in accordance with the maker's instructions, among which it is important to note that an independent battery must be used. Do not connect the Strobelight to the battery on the motor-cycle.

Check the right-side cylinder first. Start the engine and run it at a speed which will ensure the auto-advance mechanism has set the ignition in the fully advanced position. On models fitted with a revolution counter, this speed will be not less than 3,250 r.p.m.

Now project the flashing beam from the Strobelight through the chaincase aperture, when the marker line will appear to become stationary and, if the timing is correct, will be exactly opposite the pointer.

If adjustment is required, slacken the upper contact-breaker screws *A* and *B*, Fig. 37, and turn the eccentric pin *C* one way or the other until the above condition is obtained. Note that a great advantage of this method is that the ignition timing can be adjusted while the engine is running. Re-tighten the screws *A* and *B* and repeat the operation for the lower pair of the contact points.

VALVE CLEARANCES

It is advisable to check valve clearances at intervals of about 2,000 miles although if the valve mechanism is running quietly, a longer interval will suffice. The engine must be quite cold for this operation and for most twin cylinder engines described in this book, the clearances must be 0·008 in. (inlet) and 0·010 in. (exhaust). Sports engines, i.e. those with two carburettors, can be run at 0·010 in. and 0·012 in. respectively when used for competition purposes, because of the higher temperatures involved.

Excessive clearances will reduce the valve lift and cause late opening of the valves, resulting in mechanical clatter and loss of efficiency. Insufficient clearances may result in loss of compression and power, and perhaps burning of the exhaust valves in bad cases. In addition to routine checks,

GENERAL MAINTENANCE 77

the clearances should be examined at 250 miles from new and after grinding-in the valves.

Adjusting the Clearances. Construction of the rocker assembly has remained unchanged since 1962 and the following notes apply to all engines.

While it is possible to re-set valve clearances without disturbing the petrol tank, it will considerably simplify the task if the tank is taken off. There is no necessity to drain it—just turn off the taps and disconnect the pipes. Remove the cross strap beneath the front of the tank (not all models have this fitment) and unscrew the fixing nut exposed after the rubber grommet has been extracted from the tank top. Note carefully the order in which the various components which comprise the tank fixing are assembled, because they must be reassembled in the same sequence to avoid any metal-to-metal contact. In fact, the whole tank is insulated from the frame by rubber. Lift the tank off, taking great care not to scrape its enamel on the steering yoke.

Remove the sparking plugs to allow the engine to be turned easily by hand (using the starter pedal) without resistance due to compression, and take off the one-piece rocker cover and gasket. If the last item shows signs of leakage, or is damaged, it should be replaced by a new one.

The valve clearance is measured at the gap between the valve stem and the rocker, and because of the special cam design on B.S.A. twin cylinder engines, it is most important that you adopt the procedure given below for checking or adjusting the clearances.

To check, say, the right-side inlet valve clearance, rotate the engine slowly by means of the starter pedal until the left-side inlet valve is fully open (i.e. the rocker arm for that particular valve is fully depressed). This is the correct position for checking the right-side inlet valve. Similarly to check the left-side inlet valve clearance, turn the engine gently until the right-side inlet valve is fully open. Adopt the same procedure for the two exhaust valves.

Check the gap with a feeler gauge and if re-setting is necessary, release the locknut (Fig. 42), and adjust the screw until the gap is just sufficient for the appropriate feeler gauge to enter. Hold the adjusting screw stationary and firmly tighten the locknut against the rocker arm face. Check the clearance again.

DECARBONIZING AND VALVE GRINDING

The removal of carbon deposits and the subjection of the engine to a "top overhaul" is quite a straightforward operation, but should only be undertaken when the engine really needs it. This is indicated in several ways, such as a gradual decline in the power output, especially noticeable on hills; an increased tendency to "pinking" (a metallic tapping when under load); a tendency for the engine to run hotter than usual; and a flatness in the exhaust note.

It is seldom necessary to remove the barrel, unless it is felt that the piston or gudgeon pin require attention.

The picture is a little different with engines used for competition purposes, because here the need for removal of the cylinder head is much more

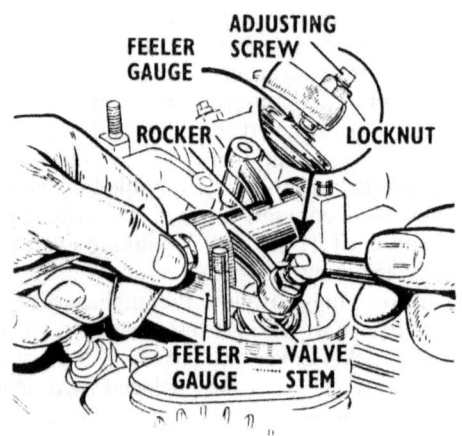

Fig 42   Making an adjustment to the valve clearances

Because of special quietening ramps on the cams it is important to follow the sequence of operations given in the text, otherwise the clearances may be incorrectly adjusted.

likely to be due to the condition of the valves, which are subject to considerable stress at high engine speeds. In particular, if maximum safe engine r.p.m. has been exceeded, the valves should be regarded with suspicion.

Preliminary Work. To allow plenty of space in which to work, it will be advisable to remove the petrol tank and then both side panels to give added clearance for the carburettors. Turn off the taps and unscrew the pipe connections. Remove the anti-roll bar across the front of the underside of the tank (on earlier models this takes the form of a plain strap). This applies to steel tanks; those made of fibre-glass have the centre fixing only.

Then release the tank centre mounting assembly (concealed by a rubber grommet), at the same time taking careful note of the sequence of dismantling in order to ensure correct reassembly. The tank is completely insulated from contact with the frame by rubber mountings on the frame top tube and at the centre mounting, and when reassembling, there must not be any metal-to-metal contact between frame and tank.

GENERAL MAINTENANCE

Detach the air filter(s) from the carburettor(s). Up to 1966 screwed connections were used, but thereafter the filters were attached by clips and flexible connections. Before the filters are reassembled to the carburettors, clean them in accordance with the details on page 38.

The carburettor(s) can be removed without being dismantled and, still attached to the control cables, tied up out of the way. Check all the joint washers for soundness (these will vary in quantity and materials for different engine types), and do not hestitate to renew any which are not in perfect order. Similarly, the rubber ring on the carburettor flange must be in good condition to preserve an airtight joint. On models with a single carburettor the manifold need not be removed from the head.

Next, disconnect the high-tension leads from the sparking plugs and then unscrew the plugs from the cylinder head. Remove the engine steady bolt at the cylinder head, slacken the bolt at the frame end, and swing the steady stay to one side. Disconnect the rocker oil feed pipe at its entry to the rear of the cylinder head, but do not unscrew the union. Up to the year 1968, the pipe was tapped off the main oil return line near to the oil tank, but thereafter the connection was made at the crankcase oil pipe union in order to improve the supply to the rockers. The balance pipe fitted between the inlet ports on later (two carburettor) models need not be disturbed.

Finally, remove the exhaust system completely. The pipes, initially, are a push fit in the cylinder head but may have become tight because of burnt oil, etc., in which case tap the pipes out of the head with a *soft* mallet. Some early models have the exhaust pipes interconnected in front of the silencers, later models have a tie-rod between the pipes in front of the cylinder head, and the latest models have interconnected pipes at the same place. These connections must also be dismantled before the exhaust systems can be removed. On models with high-level pipes, the silencers and interconnecting pipe should be removed first.

Removing the Rockers and the Cylinder Head. The rockers and their spindles are enclosed by a cast cover and after removing the six nuts, "break" the joint by a light tap with a soft mallet applied to the projections at the rear of the cover. If the gasket is imperfect in any way it must be replaced, otherwise the joint will never be oiltight. Also remove the two central studs, for which purpose a stud box will be advisable, or alternatively, two nuts locked together.

Two of the cylinder head bolts cannot be released without first dismantling the exhaust rocker assembly. Unscrew the exhaust (front) rocker arm screws until sufficient clearance is obtained to allow the two pushrods to be taken out and, after releasing the nut on the right side of the rocker spindle, drive it out towards the left side, *using a very soft mallet* to avoid damaging the threads. The exhaust rocker assemblies will then be free and can be taken out. When reassembling, it is important that the thrust washers are related correctly with the rockers (Fig. 43), to ensure that the adjusting screws are central with the valve stem, and to avoid damage to the mounting pillars. The inlet rockers need not be disturbed except for slackening the adjusting screws prior to removal of the push-rods.

The cylinder head is retained by both bolts and nuts. These must be released by *only a small amount at a time* to avoid any possible distortion of the head/barrel joint face, the best way being to ease the four bolts below the rocker spindles first, then the one inside the push-rod passageway (Fig. 44), and finally the four nuts situated in front of, and behind, the

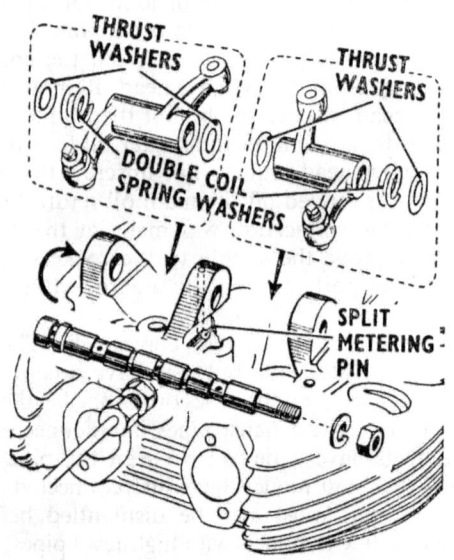

Fig 43   The correct method of assembling the rockers

The inlet rocker shaft and rockers are shown but the exhaust rocker assembly is identical. The thrust washers must be placed against the aluminium supports on the cylinder head.

sparking plugs. The head, complete with manifold where applicable, can then be lifted off the barrel, the joint being "broken" if necessary by applying a very soft mallet below the exhaust ports.

If the oil-feed union is removed, it will reveal a small metering pin which regulates the flow of oil to the rocker spindles. Check that this pin is in good order (any replacement must be of the same size) and that all oilways are clear, by testing with one of the proprietary types of pressure feed oil-can.

Cylinder Head Gasket. Examine this closely. Gas leakage, especially on the "land" between the bores, is indicated by dark patches and burnt edges round the bores. In either case, renew the gasket.

GENERAL MAINTENANCE 81

Removal of the Valves. It is always advisable to examine the valve seats when decarbonizing because it will avoid specially dismantling for this purpose at a later date. The job of removing the valves is made easy if a spring-compressing tool is used, such as B.S.A. Service Tool No. 61-3340, shown in Fig. 45. The collets fit into a tapered hole in the spring collar and as the tool begins to compress the spring, a sharp tap on the collar or spring side will jar the collets free. Continue compressing the springs until

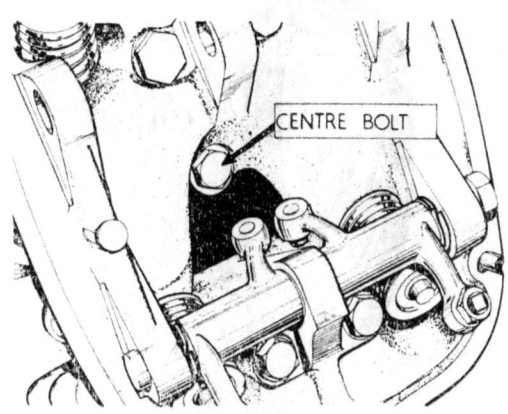

Fig 44 The cylinder head centre bolt

The centre bolt is inside the push-rod well and is inaccessible until the push-rods have been taken out. The illustration also shows the cylinder head bolts normally concealed by the exhaust rockers.

the collets can be lifted out, then unscrew the tool and remove valve and springs.

Examination of the Valves. Inspect the valve face and its seating on the cylinder head. If these are only lightly pitted, then a little fine grinding paste, obtainable from any motor accessory dealer, will restore them to their original condition (*see* page 84). If the pitting is excessive, do not attempt to regrind the valve without first having the face re-cut by a B.S.A. dealer, who has special equipment for this particular job. Alternatively, of course, you can fit a new valve, which is probably the better course because extensive re-cutting of the valve face may reduce the width at the edge to the point where it becomes liable to burning.

In addition, grinding-in an excessively pitted valve will eventually remove too much material from the seat in the cylinder head, which then becomes "pocketed" (i.e. recessed below the level of the combustion chamber surface) resulting in a deterioration of performance. This is specially important in the case of an aluminium cylinder head, where the valve seats are cast in position and cannot be renewed easily.

The Valve Springs. It is good practice to replace the valve springs whenever the engine is decarbonized. They are subjected to great stress and, particularly in the case of the exhaust valve, great heat, and tend to take a permanent set, with consequent loss of efficiency. Compare the

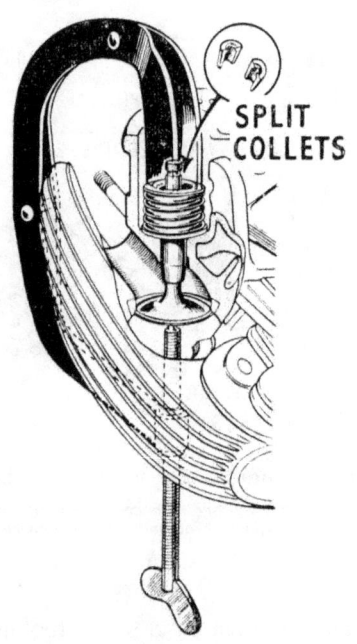

Fig 45 How to use the valve spring compressor

To avoid risk of damage to the valve head, place a small piece of soft metal, such as brass or aluminium, between the threaded shaft and the valve.

overall length of your springs with the original free lengths given in the following table and if they are shorter by more than 1/16 in. they should be replaced.

When refitting the springs on 1966–9 engines be careful to see that the outer spring has its close-wound coils inserted in the spring cup against the cylinder head. (Note: these springs have the coils closer together at one end of the spring than they are at the opposite end.)

Examination of the Valve Guides. Excessive play between valve and guide is undesirable and, if present, the guides must be replaced. The valves

GENERAL MAINTENANCE

also may be at fault, and if ridges have formed on their stems then new valves are also required.

The old guide can be driven out with a simple punch having a piloted end to fit the bore, such as B.S.A. Service Tool 61-3382. Because of the differing expansion rates between the guides and the cylinder head, it will assist in removal of the guides if the cylinder head is first immersed in very hot water. This will not only make extraction easier, but also help to prevent scoring of the soft surface of guide hole in the cylinder head. It is equally important to heat the cylinder head before inserting the new guides,

VALVE SPRING DIMENSIONS

Model	Years	Inner Spring Length	Outer Spring Length
All	1962–5	$1\frac{5}{8}$	$2\frac{1}{32}$
A50W only	1966	$1\frac{1}{2}$	$1\frac{5}{8}$
All	1966–9	$1\frac{7}{16}$	$1\frac{3}{4}$

which must be driven in from the top with the same tool mentioned above, until the shoulder prevents further insertion. For 1967–9 engines the guides are of a non-ferrous material having greater expansion properties, but the same comments apply. Before 1967 the guides were of cast iron.

When the new guides are in position, it is essential that the valve seats in the head are *refaced with a valve seat cutter* to make certain that the bore of the guide and the seat are concentric with each other. Suitable tools for this task are available as B.S.A. Service Tools Nos. 61-3301 (cutter); 61-3293 (pilot); and 61-3290 (holder), from any B.S.A. Service dealer.

Decarbonizing the Cylinder Head and Pistons. This is a straightforward job although calling for care in carrying it out. Rotate the engine carefully by means of the starter pedal until the pistons are at the top of their stroke and then seal the push-rod passageway with a clean cloth to prevent carbon chippings from entering. A proprietary scraper or even an *old blunt*, knife or screwdriver may be used to remove carbon from the piston crowns. Great care is needed to avoid marking the surface, which should be smooth and undamaged. It is as well to leave any slight carbon deposits on the edges of the pistons as an aid to economy in oil consumption.

The cylinder head ports can then be dealt with and, as with the pistons, care must be taken to avoid damaging the valve seats and sparking plug threads with the decarbonizing tool. All trace of carbon must be removed to leave the surfaces smooth and unmarked.

Remember that all the surfaces coated with a deposit of carbon are made of aluminium, a soft material which will suffer damage easily and it is well to "make haste slowly" using all the patience you can muster. (Note: never use a solution of caustic soda to dissolve the carbon—it will also attack the aluminium.)

Finally, rotate the engine until the pistons are at the bottom of the bores and wipe away all loose carbon from inside the bores. Similarly, clean the valve guide bores and sparking plug threads.

Grinding-in the Valves. Grinding with a fine-grade compound should be sufficient to give good mating surfaces between valve and seat, and hence a good gas seal. If the seats do not warrant re-cutting by machine but, nevertheless, are in poor condition, use a coarse grade of compound before finishing with fine grade. Carefully wipe away all trace of the coarse paste before changing over.

Smear a small quantity of paste evenly round the face of the valve, but before returning it to its seat, add a light spring under its head. When hand pressure is released at intervals during grinding, the spring will raise the head of the valve and allow it to be rotated to a new position.

A special tool incorporating a suction cup at one end (Fig. 46), B.S.A. Service Tool No. 61-5035, must be pressed on to the valve head to enable this to be rotated backwards and forwards, while at the same time maintaining a light downward pressure. This means, of course, that if the method shown in the illustration is followed the hands will slowly slide down the handle, and when they are brought to the top again to repeat the process the valve can be turned to a new position.

Continue the grinding procedure until a uniformly matt surface is evident all round the valve and the seat.

It is of the utmost importance to wash away all traces of grinding compound, because if any remains after reassembly, it is liable to find its way into the cylinders, with consequent rapid wear.

Replacing the Valves. First check that the valve spring collar is in place against the cylinder head. Add a little engine oil to the valve stem and replace in position, complete with springs and top collar. Using the spring-compressing tool (Fig. 45), close the springs until the split collets can be inserted. The exposed end of the valve stem should be greased to assist in retaining the collets as the spring is released. Check that the collets are properly seated.

On 1966-9 engines, the valve springs are of a different type from those fitted before that time, in that the coils at one end of the spring are closer together than those at the opposite end. These springs must be assembled with the close coils downwards, i.e. against the cylinder head.

Removing the O.H. Rockers. The exhaust rockers have already been removed to give access to two cylinder head bolts and the inlet rockers are

GENERAL MAINTENANCE

removed in the same manner. When replacing, return the spindles to their own positions and reassemble the rockers and their washers in the correct sequence (*see* Fig. 43 and "Cylinder head removal," page 79).

Removing the Cylinder Block. Normally there is no necessity to remove the block; the only circumstances which require this are those which indicate poor condition of the pistons, rings, and cylinder bores. Excessively

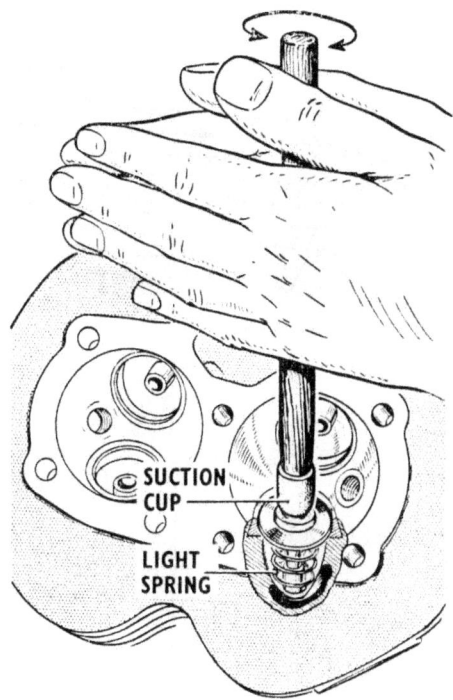

Fig 46   Grinding-in valves

The purpose of the small spring below the valve head is to cause the valve to lift off its seat when downward pressure is released. This simplifies turning the head to a new position.

worn rings, or bores, or damage due to seizure, may be indicated by one or more of several symptoms such as heavy oil consumption (voluminous blue smoke from the exhaust), excessive piston tap when the engine is hot and reduced compression.

Be wary of the last item, however, because it is much more likely to be caused by faulty valves which may require regrinding, or even renewing, if burnt. This subject is covered in the section "Grinding-in the Valves" (page 84).

Worn rings may account for excessive piston tap, but (and this is more likely to be the cause) may also be due to worn cylinder bores. This can be checked without removing the block, if the engine is turned until both pistons are at the bottom of the stroke, when the bores will be exposed for examination and measurement (*see* following section).

If it is decided to remove the block, check that the pistons are still at the bottom of the bores and remove all the nuts from round the base flange—using a ring spanner, not the usual open-ended type. A sharp

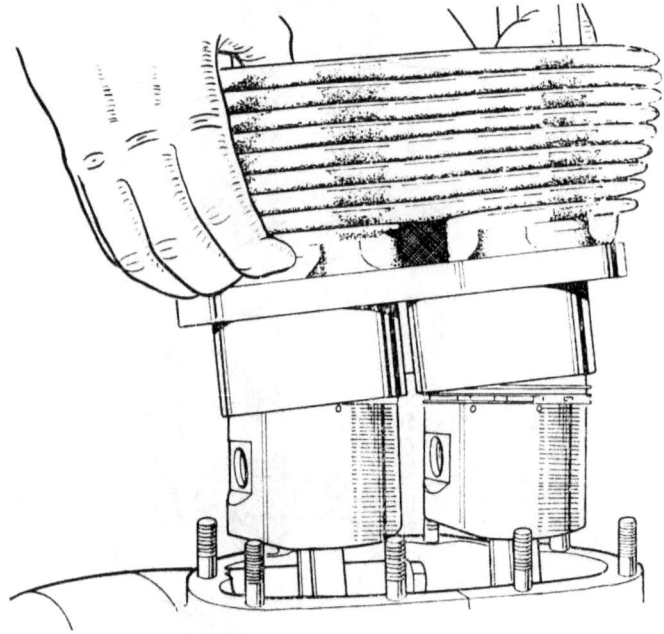

Fig 47   Raising the cylinder block from the crankcase

Both hands are required to lift the block because of its weight, and the illustration shows how it is possible for the pistons to be damaged on the crankcase studs and other parts, unless there is an assistant available to help.

upward tap on the block with the palm of the hand should separate it from the crankcase. Do not use a mallet for fear of breaking the fins. Now, gently lift the block upwards until the pistons emerge from the bores (Fig. 47) and here it will be as well to have an assistant to steady the pistons, in order to avoid any possible damage through contact with the connecting rod or crankcase mouth, etc. The block is heavy and needs care to draw it aside for placing on the bench. The tappets are retained in the block by circlips at their upper ends and will not fall out.

Now cover the whole of the crankcase mouth with clean cloth to keep out foreign matter while the block and, perhaps later the pistons, receive attention.

If the gasket between the cylinder base flange and the crankcase face was stuck to either of these surfaces, carefully scrape off the remnants. Remember that the crankcase is made of a soft material and great care must be taken not to score the surface.

Examination of the Cylinder Block. Inspect each bore carefully for wear, which will be most apparent at the top, in the form of a ridge at the end of the piston travel in the direction of its thrust, i.e. at the front and at the back of each bore. The bottom of the bore usually wears by a negligible amount and if this is taken as a reference size, the maximum permissibl wear at the ridge is 0·010 in. increase on the reference diameter. In the absence of any suitable measuring instrument (and this is usually specialist equipment), take the barrel to a B.S.A. dealer for advice.

Scoring of the bores automatically means re-boring the block, and shiny marks on the surface should be treated with suspicion, because they are most likely caused by piston seizure and hence attention may be necessary to the pistons.

Blocks can be re-bored by arrangement with your local B.S.A. dealer, who can then supply suitable oversize pistons. Note that B.S.A. manufacture two oversizes only, i.e. $\frac{1}{2}$ mm and 1 mm.

Removing the Pistons. This operation is required only if further dismantling is being carried out or if the pistons require replacement due, perhaps, to damage following a seizure, although in this case, provided that the area of seizure is small, light filing of the high spot with a smooth file may be sufficient to restore the piston to a satisfactory condition. *This must not be overdone.*

First prise out one gudgeon pin circlip from each piston with the aid of a suitably pointed tool inserted into the notch provided for this purpose. Discard these circlips and fit new ones at the appropriate time.

The gudgeon pin will be tight in the piston and the latter must be warmed before any attempt is made to remove the pin. A good method is to stand an electric iron on the piston crown until this condition is achieved. With the piston thoroughly warm, draw out the gudgeon pin from the side without the circlip, using an extractor tool such as that shown in Fig. 48. Alternatively, tap out the gudgeon pin with a flat-ended punch and a light hammer, at the same time supporting the piston on the opposite side in order to avoid any risk of bending the connecting rod due to heavy side loading. If the pistons are to be refitted, mark them on the inside of the skirt with the letter F to indicate the front and with L or R to record the side of the engine from which they were removed. This will enable them to be reassembled in the same bores and the same way round as originally fitted

Piston Rings. Any discoloration on the faces of the piston rings is an indication that they have not been in proper contact with the cylinder walls. There should be a smooth, metallic surface all the way round and, in this case, the rings do not require attention.

When free from the pistons, the rings should possess a certain amount of "springiness" and a gap of about 3/16 in. Renew any ring which has lost its tension and has a smaller gap.

When in position, all rings must be free in their grooves with an absolute minimum of up-and-down clearance. If they are stuck in the grooves

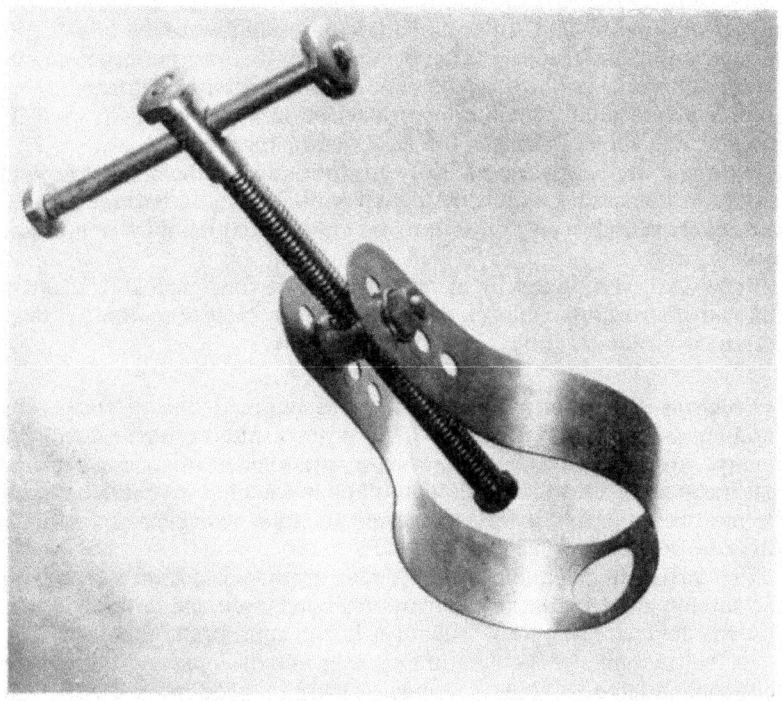

Fig 48 A proprietary tool for removing or inserting the gudgeon pin
Provision is made on this tool for various sizes of gudgeon pins. Different pressure pads are carried on the ends of the tommy bar and on the pressure screw.

brush with plenty of paraffin and gently prise them out. Clear all carbon from the grooves and from behind the rings. A piece of old broken ring sharpened to a chisel edge can be used for clearing the groove. Fortunately, modern oils seldom lead to this state of affairs, and are one of the reasons why you should keep to one of the brands listed on page 42.

GENERAL MAINTENANCE

It is not an easy task to remove or replace rings and great care is needed because they are brittle and will withstand only a limited amount of expansion. The safest way is to insert short strips of sheet metal, as shown in Fig. 49, and ease the rings off very gently. Note that the second piston ring has a taper face which is difficult to detect visually. It is marked with a letter "T" on its upper face and it must be fitted with its "T"-face to the top. If it is fitted in the wrong manner the oil consumption will be heavy, accompanied by blue smoke from the exhaust, and the engine will have to be dismantled again to rectify the error.

The rings can be checked for wear by placing them in the lower part of the bore from which they were removed. Each must be "squared-up" by

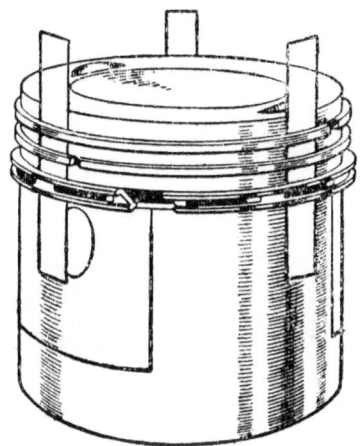

Fig 49 A good method for removing or fitting piston rings

Three strips are essential. Approximate sizes are ⅜ in. wide × 2 in. long. All the rings are fragile and great care must be exercised to avoid breakage.

locating it with a piston inserted temporarily. Now measure the gap with feeler gauges (Fig. 50).

When new, the piston ring gap was 0·008–0·010 in. and provided that it does not greatly exceed this figure, the ring can be used again. Any large increase, however, say up to 0·025 in., means that the ring must be replaced.

When the rings have been refitted to the pistons, turn them round in their grooves so that their gaps are equally spaced, in order to reduce gas leakage to a minimum.

Replacing the Pistons. Each piston must be installed on the same connecting rod and the same way round as it was originally. (This was the object in marking the pistons with symbols when dismantling.) Warm the pistons as before (*see* page 87), dip the gudgeon pin in engine oil and press home, reversing the procedure used for extraction, and using the same tool (Fig. 48). It is essential to fit new circlips afterwards; omission of these will allow the gudgeon pin to move endwise and score the cylinder wall. Check also that the circlip is properly seated or the same trouble will arise.

Replacing the Block. Before commencing operations, prepare two pieces of ½ in. square wood about 8 in. long.

Place a new gasket on the face of the crankcase, which has been lightly smeared with jointing compound. Now lay the wooden strips across the

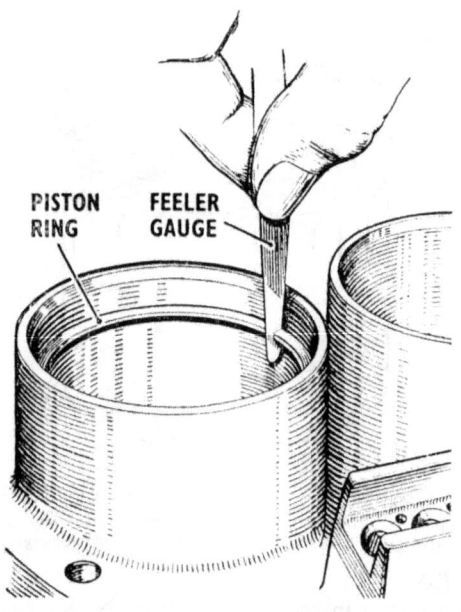

Fig 50   Checking the wear of a piston ring

Note that the ring must be parallel with the end of the cylinder bore before using a feeler gauge. This end of the bore is invariably the least worn part of the cylinder and will give a reliable check on the ring wear.

mouth of the crankcase, one behind and the other in front of the pistons (Fig. 51), the purpose of the strips being to hold the pistons parallel with the bores and to prevent them from descending into the crankcase as the barrel is lowered.

Liberally coat the pistons and rings with engine oil and space out the ring gaps equally round the piston. It will also be advisable to add "slippers" to compress the rings (Fig. 51) to make the assembly much easier. After

GENERAL MAINTENANCE

fitting the slippers, the rings must still be just free to move. Slippers are available as B.S.A. Service Tools, No. 61-3682 for the A50 engines and No. 61-3707 for A65 engines.

Coat both cylinder bores with engine oil. It will be seen from the illustration that as the block is lowered the slippers will slide down to the bottom of the piston and obviously these, and the wooden strips, can be withdrawn as soon as the rings have entered the bores. This is an operation

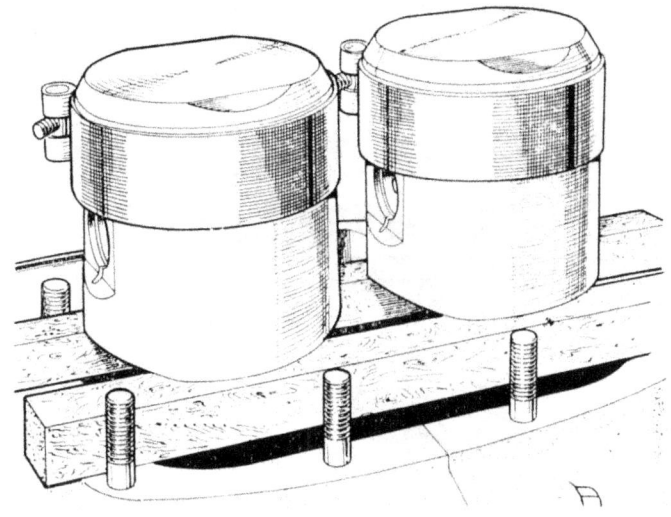

Fig 51   Replacing the cylinder block

As soon as the pistons have entered the bores and the slippers are at the bottom of the pistons, the wooden strips and the slippers can be removed. An assistant will have to support the barrel while this is being done.

which must be carried out carefully and gently and it will be as well to have the services of an assistant for this part of the rebuilding.

Replace and tighten the cylinder base nuts firmly and evenly.

Replacing the Cylinder Head. At this stage the head will have been re-assembled with its valves, springs, etc. (*see* "Replacing the Valves," page 84), and the inlet rockers, but not the exhaust rockers. These must be omitted until the head is bolted down.

Fit the cylinder head gasket with the same face against the block as originally fitted but, with a new one, this is of no consequence.

Lower the head into position and lightly tighten the bolts and nuts in rotation, as shown in Fig. 52, to ensure even distribution of pressure and freedom from distortion. Follow the same sequence two or three times tightening a little more each time, until all bolts and nuts are really tight.

It is preferable to use a torque spanner for this purpose, set at 28–30 lb ft Check the tightness again after 250 miles, but make quite sure that the engine is cold when this is done.

The way is now clear to replace the exhaust rockers and spindle, using the correct sequence as given in Fig. 43 (*see* page 79). Also replace the front centre studs for the rocker cover.

Replace the push-rods, the two longest ones operating the exhaust rockers. Make sure that the lower end of each rod is correctly seated on its tappet (the rods will be seen to rise and fall with the rotation of the camshaft if the engine is turned gently) and insert in turn the appropriate

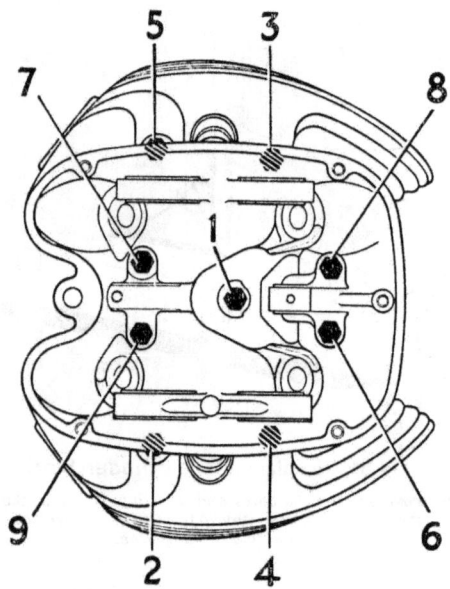

Fig 52 The order of tightening the cylinder head bolts

These bolts or nuts must be tightened down before the exhaust rockers or push rods are replaced, otherwise bolts numbered 1, 7, and 9 will be inaccessible. For the 1967–9 models the two bolts at positions 6 and 8 were changed to ⅜ in. dia × 20 T.P.I. B.S.F. threads tapped ⅝ in. deep, and older models can be converted if required. Counterbore and remove the first thread.

rocker ball-end into the cup at the top of the push-rod. Screw up the valve-clearance adjusters to give an approximately correct clearance and when all are positioned, set the valve clearances accurately as detailed in the section, "Valve Clearances," page 76.

Return the rocker cover joint washer (lightly smeared with a little jointing compound) to the joint face and add the cover. Excessive tightening of the nuts must be avoided because of risk of damage to the cover.

Reconnect the oil feed pipe to the rocker spindles. Clean and adjust

GENERAL MAINTENANCE 93

the sparking plugs (*see* page 67), as required. After replacement *make sure* that the h.t. cables are correctly connected.

Notes on Final Assembly. The carburettor(s) may now be bolted to the inlet manifold, or ports, as the case may be. Do not omit the gaskets, which should have been renewed if showing any signs of damage. If not in good condition, air leaks may ensue, so interfering with correct carburation.

Next, dismantle and clean the air filter(s), in accordance with the details given on page 37. The screw-on type used from 1962–5 will need extra care when fitting because the fine thread is easily damaged (*see* page 38).

Now refit the exhaust system, making sure that the pipes are well home in the cylinder head before attempting to tighten their anchorage bolts, etc.

As already mentioned in the early stages of dismantling, the petrol tank is entirely insulated from the frame by various rubber pads and every care must be taken to see that these are properly fitted and to ensure that there is no metal-to-metal contact between tank and frame. If this happens it will not be long before you have a leaking tank.

Remaining parts, such as the tank strap, steady stay, petrol pipes, side panels, etc., may now be added and the engine started up for a trial run.

VALVE TIMING

The camshaft, which controls the valve timing, is driven from the crankshaft by gears which are keyed to their shafts. It is impossible for the valve timing to alter and the only occasion on which the gears need to be disturbed is when the engine is being dismantled, or for some other special reason.

In this event, it will be necessary to remove the timing covers to expose the gears, which lie behind the inner (or sandwich) cover. To take off the outer cover, first remove the starter and gear-change pedals followed by the three retaining screws (their heads require the use of the correct type of screwdriver) when the contact-breaker unit, starter pedal spring, clutch-operating lever, and gear-change centralizing spring will be exposed.

Press down the clutch-lever, making sufficient slack in the cable for it to be disconnected and drawn out through the back of the case. A quick-release device was introduced into the clutch cable, at engine numbers A65-1307, and A50-396 in 1962, which enabled the cable to be changed readily at any time without dismantling the covers. Swing the lever outwards and extract the plunger and ball. Note the position of the arm on the starter spring retaining plate for reassembly purposes, and prise the plate off the shaft, followed by the spring. Finally, withdraw the gear-change spring and stop plate. On 1962–3 models the stop plate was retained by a key, but in 1964 a change was made to the use of a small screw to secure the plate to its spindle and the screw must be slackened before taking off the plate.

To remove the inner cover, if a rev-counter is fitted, take off the cable drive housing on the front of the cover and take out the spindle. Removal of eight screws will finally release the cover. Do not take out the rearmost screw, because this is the anchorage point for the starter pedal spring and does not effect cover removal. Tap the cover gently with a mallet to "break" the joint and pull the cover away. The contact-breaker leads will still be attached, but for working on the timing gears only, there is no necessity to disconnect these leads.

The timing gears will now be exposed and can be examined as required. If they are to be removed, tackle the camshaft gear first. Flatten the tab

Fig 53   The timing gear marks

The pencils indicate the positions of the marks on the gears at the root of the teeth. Note the position of the dot on the engine shaft pinion in relation to the keyway in the thread.

washer and unscrew the nut, taking great care to avoid damaging the crankcase. The pinion can then be drawn off the shaft with a B.S.A. Service Tool No. 61-3676, a multi-purpose extractor.

The engine shaft pinion will require prior removal of the crankshaft nut and the oil pump worm, *both of which have a left-hand thread and must be turned clockwise to unscrew*. For this pinion too, the same extractor fitted with different legs is suitable.

Now comes the most important feature of this operation. When reassembling, the timing marks on the pinions (located at the root of the teeth) must be in accordance with those given in Fig. 53, otherwise you

GENERAL MAINTENANCE 95

may suffer from a variety of troubles such as poor performance, high fuel consumption, and other faults.

The remainder of the reassembly is straightforward, but it may be as well to fit a new gasket between the inner cover and the crankcase and to thoroughly grease the clutch thrust ball and plunger when re-fitting.

CARE OF THE TRANSMISSION

Clutch Control Adjustment. The clutch cable must never be adjusted to eliminate all slackness; there must always be about 1/16 in. of free play in the cable as measured at the handlebar lever.

It will be readily understood that if there is no play at all there will be a tendency for the clutch plates to remain slightly separated and hence there will be a certain amount of clutch slip. This will cause overheating of the clutch, and eventually excessive wear of the friction pads. On the other hand, if the figure is greatly exceeded the travel of the clutch disengagement mechanism will be reduced and hence the clutch plates will not separate properly, causing difficult and noisy gear engagement and unnecessary wear and tear in the gearbox.

When further adjustment becomes necessary, this must be made at the clutch itself. Unscrew the inspection cap near the rear of the primary chaincase to expose the adjuster nut and locknut at the centre of the pressure plate. On 1962-5 engines this inspection cap is concealed by a second cap, oval in shape, which covers two inspection caps and the rear of these is the one to be removed.

To make an adjustment, first slacken off the cable adjuster at the handlebar. Then release the lock-nut (Fig. 54), and turn the screw in a clockwise direction until all the cable slackness has been *just* taken up, using only light pressure with the screwdriver. If the adjuster screw is now slackened off about ¾ turn and the locknut tightened, this will give satisfactory working clearance at the control lever in the timing case (Fig. 55). Final cable adjustment can be made at the handlebar lever.

If you feel it is necessary to examine the control lever, take off the timing cover and remove the thrust plunger and ball from the crankcase (*see* "Valve Timing," page 93). The end of the rod thus exposed must be flat and should be replaced if indented to any extent. If the ball appears to be defective (e.g. flat surfaces or pitting) replace it with another of 7/32 in. diameter. Smear the ball, plunger and fulcrum with grease when reassembling.

Clutch Cable. Because of the difficulty experienced with very early models in replacing the clutch cable without first dismantling the timing case, etc., a quickly detachable connection (Fig. 56), was introduced in 1962 at engine numbers A50-396 and A65-1307. If the cable is intact, it will first be necessary to uncouple the handlebar connection to provide sufficient slack to operate the detachable connection. When fitting the

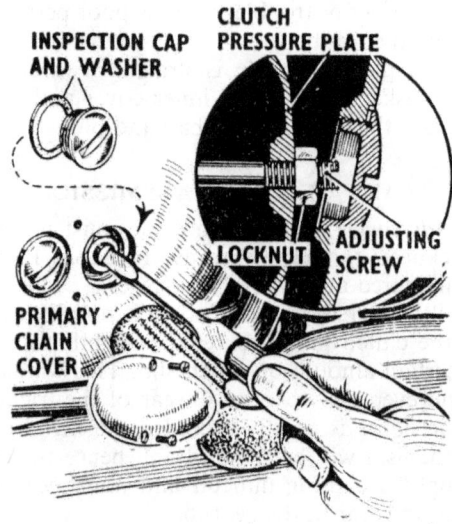

Fig 54 The main clutch adjustment from the chaincase side

The oval cover, enclosing two inspection caps, was discontinued from 1966, when the front inspection cap (used for adjusting the clutch springs) was no longer fitted.

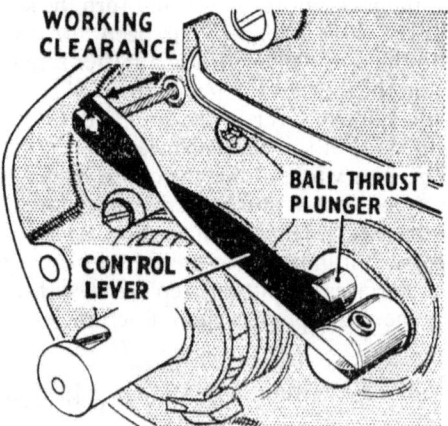

Fig 55 Clutch lever adjustment (inside the timing case)

The normal adjustment is from the opposite side of the machine. All that is required here is a satisfactory working clearance of $\frac{1}{16}$ in. to make sure the control lever does not foul the timing cover when the clutch is engaged.

GENERAL MAINTENANCE

new cable, carry out assembly at the detachable connector first and complete the fitting of the cable at the handlebar lever.

To release the cable, first draw back the rubber sleeve and pull out the adapter (slotted to simplify removal), followed by the abutment. The cable nipple can then be taken out of the connector, leaving this item and its spring still in position.

A lubricator was introduced into the cable in 1969 and grease should be applied at regular intervals to ensure ease of operation.

Primary Chain Adjustment (General). All engines are built in unit construction with the gearbox and employ a triple-row primary chain which is *not* fitted with a spring link.

While it is undesirable to have a slack chain, with consequent wear of the sprocket teeth and the chain itself, it is even more undesirable to run with the chain too tight because this will cause not only the above troubles

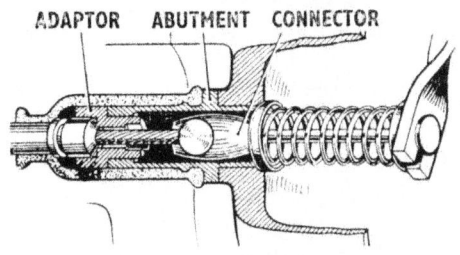

Fig 56 The quickly-detachable clutch cable components

but also heavy loading of engine and gearbox bearings. The chain should have $\frac{1}{8}-\frac{1}{4}$ in. of play and a slipper-type tensioner is provided for adjustment, operating on the lower run of the chain. Adjustment can be made without taking off the chaincase cover.

Primary Chain Adjustment (1962–5 *Engines*). The adjuster, projecting from the bottom of the chaincase and locked by a cap nut, comprises a hollow, screwed sleeve in the top of which a sliding thrust button bears against the chain slipper (Fig. 57).

Remove the cap nut and "feel" the thrust button with a rod of suitable diameter inserted into the adjuster. The button can then be moved up and down with a finger operating the end of the rod, the amount of movement giving the slackness in the chain.

If the slackness is excessive, screw the sleeve a little further into the chaincase, insert the rod, and again check the up and down movement of the rod. When the play in the chain falls within the limits given above, replace and tighten the cap nut. A special sealing washer is fitted above the cap nut to prevent oil leakage from the case and must not be omitted.

Primary Chain Adjustment (1966–9 *Engines*). The chain slackness must be estimated at the top run of the chain by feeling it with the fingers through the oil filler cap aperture. If adjustment is necessary, remove the cap nut as on the earlier models and then screw the adjuster in or out as required by means of the square machined on the end. With these models, the thrust button is combined with the adjuster and there is no provision for a feeler rod. It is essential to replace the special sealing washer above the cap nut to preserve an oiltight joint.

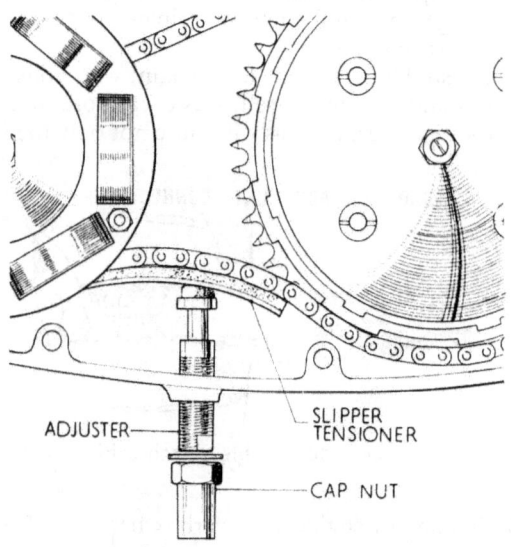

Fig 57   Adjustment of the primary chain

The plunger, bearing on the slipper tensioner, was free within the screwed adjuster on earlier models. It later became part of the adjuster itself.

Adjusting the Clutch Spring Pressure. Only after an appreciable mileage has been covered will the clutch springs require adjustment, in order to restore the pressure which will have been reduced by wear of the plates.

It is preferable to remove the primary chain cover (although on the 1962–5 engines a special aperture is provided in the case for access to the nuts—*see* Fig. 58), because adjustment of the sleeve nuts (Fig. 59), is made so much easier and also because the plates must be examined and if necessary re-set for true-running. This operation cannot be done from outside the case. Note the positions of the two red screws which are for oil level and drainage purposes (*see* page 52), and the varying lengths and positions of the other screws which retain the cover.

GENERAL MAINTENANCE 99

Normally each nut should be tightened by the same amount precisely assuming that the plates already run truly, but after this has been done, de-clutch and operate the starter pedal a few times, when it will be obvious if the plates "wobble." This is a condition which will give clutch drag and noisy gear engagement.

To give true running, readjust one or more of the nuts, either inwards or outwards, until each spring gives the same pressure, when the plates will run truly. Note that the nuts have a projection under the head to prevent

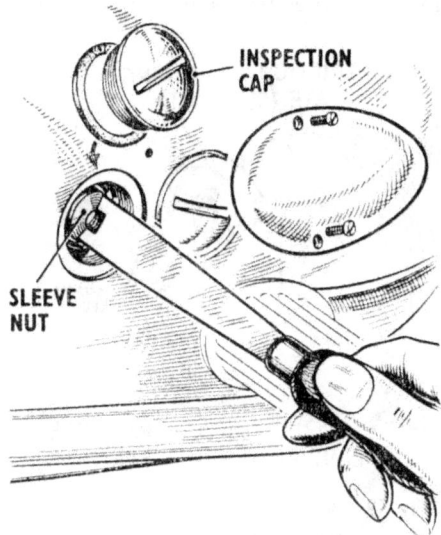

Fig 58   Access to the clutch springs through the chaincase cover

This is possible only on those models with the oval inspection cover, which conceals both spring adjustment and clutch adjustment inspection caps. All other models require the chaincase cover to be removed. This is the best way because the clutch-plates can be checked for true running at the same time.

them from working loose and this may cause some difficulty if it is necessary to slacken the screws and, in fact, if excessive force is used, the spring may be damaged and will have to be replaced.

On 1962–5 models the clutches carried five friction plates compressed by four springs, but for the 1966–9 models six friction plates were employed, with three springs for compression.

Resist the temptation to increase the spring pressure by an excessive amount, to make sure of freedom from clutch slip; this should not be overdone, otherwise operation of the clutch control will be hard work for the left hand, particularly in heavy traffic. The opposite also applies, of course, and if the sleeve nuts are not screwed up sufficiently, there will be the possibility of clutch slip.

Examination of the Clutch-plates. All B.S.A. twin-cylinder engines are fitted with multi-plate clutches, i.e. they are made up of a series of alternating plain and friction plates. The friction plates are of steel and carry segments of special friction material bonded in position. Eventually, after a great mileage, these segments will become worn to the point of replacement.

After removing the primary chaincase (*see* "Adjusting the Clutch Spring Pressure, page 98), the clutch assembly is exposed. Unscrew the sleeve nuts (Fig. 59), and remove the pressure plate complete with cups and springs.

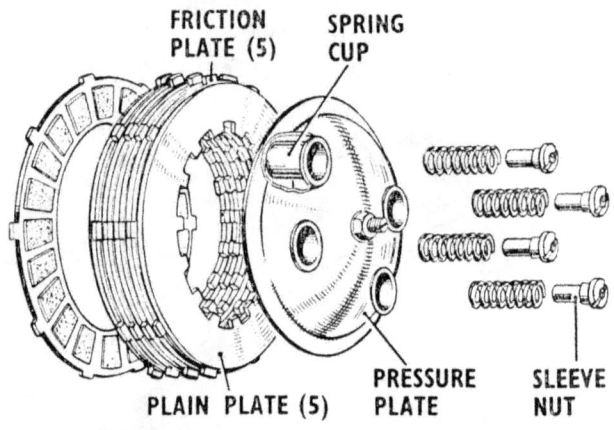

Fig 59 An exploded view of the clutch

The illustration applies to the 1962–5 models. Later models were similar except for the use of six plates and three springs only.

In removing the nuts the springs may be damaged by the projections under the heads of the nuts, in which case new springs will be required.

Extract the plates, which are a sliding fit on either the hub of the clutch, or the chainwheel, according to type. The innermost plain plate on 1962–5 engines is a tight fit on the hub and should not be disturbed unless it is absolutely necessary.

Examine all plates carefully. The segments on the friction plates must not be displaced or damaged in any way. Measure the overall width and if this is reduced to the minimum permissible thinness of 0·11 in., replace the plates, even if they are otherwise in good order. The tongues on the edges of the plates must be free from burrs and be a sliding fit in the slots in the chainwheel. These, in turn, must be smoothed with a fine file.

Check the plain plates for flatness by laying on a thick sheet of glass. If a plate can be tilted to one side, it is buckled and must be replaced. Also examine its surface for score marks: if these exist to any appreciable extent then, again, the remedy is to renew the plate.

GENERAL MAINTENANCE 101

When reassembling the clutch on 1962-5 models, insert a friction plate first (a plain steel plate is already a fixture in the chainwheel—*see* page 100), followed by alternating steel and friction plates of which there are five of each (excluding the fixed steel plate).

On 1966-9 models, there is no fixed inner plain plate and the first friction plate to be inserted bears on the inner face of the chainwheel, to be followed by alternating steel and friction plates, of which, in this case, there are six of each type.

The final (outer) plate must always be a plain one; if this is not so, then the sequence of assembly is wrong. Refit the pressure plate, springs and sleeve nuts.

If any parts have been replaced, the clutch adjustment will certainly require re-setting (*see* "Clutch Control Adjustment," page 95), and similarly spring pressures will require adjustment to provide true-running plates (*see* "Adjusting the Clutch Spring Pressure," page 98).

Since the chaincase cover was removed at the beginning of the operation, when it is reassembled and the machine is ready for the road, *remember to replenish the chaincase with oil* (*see* page 92).

Dismantling the Clutch. It is not possible to remove the clutch alone because the triple-row primary chain is not fitted with a detachable link and cannot be disconnected. Hence to remove the clutch it will also be necessary to remove the generator and then the engine sprocket, chain and clutch chainwheel as a unit. It is also one of the few dismantling jobs which will be simplified if you have the services of an assistant.

Firstly, the chain must not be under tension and the adjusting screw below the case must be slackened off until the tensioner is completely free from the chain.

Both the generator rotor nut and the clutch hub nut are tightly screwed up and the transmission must be locked up to prevent movement while the nuts are being released. Begin work at the crankshaft, leaving the clutch till last.

Engage a gear and have your assistant apply the rear brake. This will leave both of *your* hands free. Straighten the locking washer under the crankshaft nut, which can then be unscrewed. Take off the three stator nuts and washers (later models have self-locking nuts at this point). This is the stationary part of the generator and, on models up to 1966, was mounted on three studs projecting from the crankcase. For the 1967 season the stator fitted into an independent centralizing housing, but from 1968 the housing is integral with the crankcase. Carefully draw the stator off its studs, taking great care not to damage the windings of the coils. There is no necessity to disconnect the generator leads. Draw the rotor off the crankshaft and extract the key. Now turn your attention to the clutch. Dismantle and remove all the plates as described in the section "Examination of the Clutch Plates" (page 100), and draw the push-rod from the centre of the gearbox mainshaft.

Once again have your assistant apply the rear brake firmly, with a gear engaged. Straighten the locking washer under the central nut, which must then be removed.

The way is now clear for the removal of the two sprockets and the chain. Two extractors will be required. For the clutch, B.S.A. Service Tool No. 61-1912 is essential to draw the centre sleeve off the taper mainshaft and the tool is shown in operation in Fig. 60. The key need not be removed.

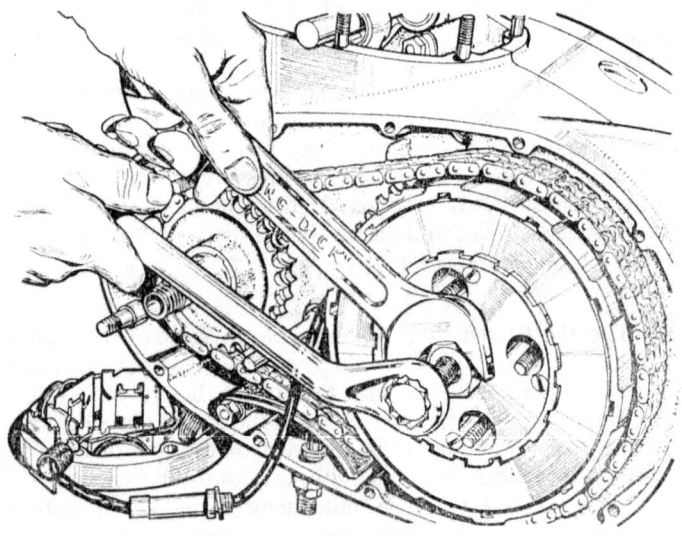

Fig 60   Using the clutch extractor tool

It will be seen that the generator leads pass between the upper and lower runs of the chain. Remember this when reassembling, otherwise everything will have to be dismantled again.

Leaving the clutch parts loose on the mainshaft, draw the engine sprocket off the crankshaft. All models from 1963–9 have tapped holes for extraction purposes in conjunction with B.S.A. Service Tool No. 61-3676, using two bolts ¼ in. diameter × 26 T.P.I. × 3 in. long.

Now withdraw the engine sprocket, clutch parts, and primary chain as a unit (Fig. 61).

If you suspect that the shock-absorber rubbers (inside the clutch hub) require attention take out the four countersunk-head screws (three on later models) and prise off the plate. With the continual variation in loading of these rubbers they may show signs of deterioration, and in this event they must be replaced. When refitting new rubbers it will be found beneficial to insert them after lubricating with liquid soap. The shape of these rubbers has varied over the years but the current components are

GENERAL MAINTENANCE 103

suitable for past years. The plate-fixing screws should receive a thin coating of "Locitite" before re-assembly. Tighten firmly.

Notes on Reassembling the Clutch. Check the chainwheel bearing for up-and-down play. A slight amount only is permissible and if this is exceeded renew the roller bearings. Twenty-one of these were used on the 1962–5 engines and twenty for 1966–9. Grease the sleeve roller tracks

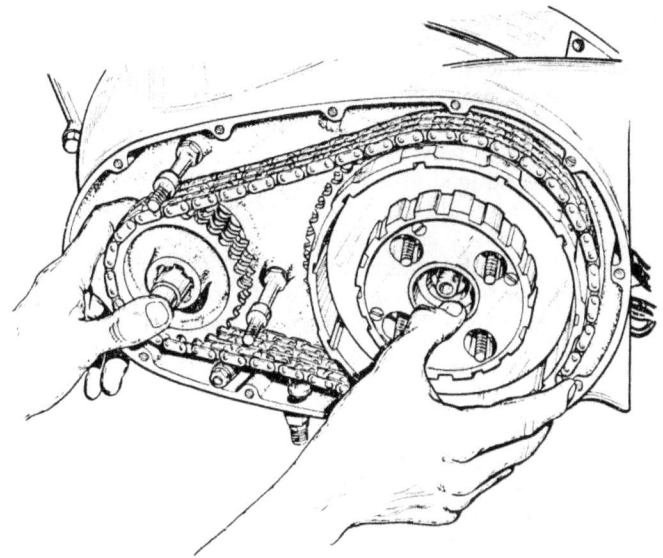

Fig 61   Taking off the primary chain
The chain must be removed and replaced complete with engine sprocket and partly dismantled clutch.

thoroughly before fitting the rollers (this will help to retain them while assembling, as well as to lubricate them when running), and slide the chainwheel over the rollers.

Take up the clutch hub completely assembled with rubbers, backplate (1962–5 models only), etc., insert the spring bolts from the rear and slide the assembly into the chainwheel.

When the crankshaft sprocket was pulled off its shaft, there may have been shims (very thin washers) in addition to the standard spacing collar. The shims were fitted in the first place to give accurate chain alignment and these and the collar should now be fitted.

Lay the partly-assembled clutch chainwheel and engine sprocket side by side on a bench (if the chainwheel is carelessly handled, it will disintegrate, scattering the rollers around your workshop), and put the chain in position round both components.

Pick up the assembled sprockets and chain as a unit (Fig. 61) and just before sliding the sprockets on to their shaft once again obtain the services of your assistant, who must pass the stator through the chain because the stator has to be fitted last.

Complete the fitting of the sprockets on to the shafts and lock the clutch chainwheel in position, first fitting the spacing collar (with its recess outwards) and then a new locking washer, followed by the nut. Tighten the nut with a torque spanner set to 65–70 lb ft.

Replace the key in the crankshaft, fit the rotor *with the Strobelight timing mark on the outside face*, and tighten the nut to a torque spanner setting of 60 lb ft. The three stator nuts require a torque setting of 5–7 lb ft and the leads are situated at the "two o'clock" position approximately. It is important that the air gap between the rotor and each stator pole piece is the same, especially with the earlier models where the stator was supported on three long studs. The gap should be 0·008/0·010 in., and if necessary the studs should be *very carefully* set over until symmetry is obtained.

Insert the clutch push-rod and reassemble the remainder of the clutch as detailed in the sections "Examination of the Clutch Plates," page 100, and "Adjusting the Clutch Spring Pressure," page 98. Readjust the chain tensioner in accordance with the instructions given in "Primary Chain Adjustment," page 97.

Rear Chain Adjustment. Most rear chains are exposed to the elements and suffer accordingly, although for the years 1962–5 rear chaincases were available at an extra charge, prolonging chain life by an appreciable margin. For this reason an exposed chain should be removed and lubricated regularly, as described on page 53. In spite of this attention, however, chains stretch as the mileage increases and the slackness must not be allowed to become excessive.

The slackness is measured at the centre of the chain run and must be actual free up-and-down play (a chain which is taut can still be strained to move up and down). The chain is at its tightest when the swinging arm is in its highest position, i.e. when the damper springs are compressed, and due allowance is made for this in the slackness figure given below, when the machine is on its stand and the damper units are extended, pushing the swinging arm to its lowest position.

With the machine in neutral gear, turn the back wheel until the position is found where the chain has its minimum amount of slackness. (This is necessary because slight variations in slackness are due to irregular wear of the chain.)

The total free movement of the chain should be $1\frac{1}{4}$ in. Where the chain is totally enclosed, the slackness can be gauged at the top run after removing the rubber inspection cap.

For 1962–5 models adjust the chain as follows. Slacken the nuts on the torque arm which links the brake cover plate to swinging arm and release

GENERAL MAINTENANCE 105

the spindle nut on the chain side of the wheel, followed by the spindle head on the opposite side. Slacken the adjuster bolt locknuts (Fig. 62, and C Fig. 65), and unscrew the bolt on the left side until the chain slackness is correct. Now unscrew the bolt on the right side (Fig. 62 and D, Fig. 65),

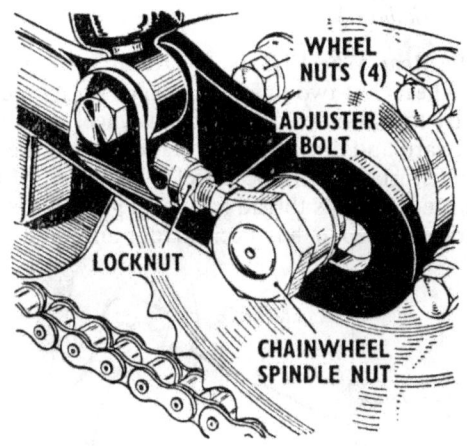

Fig 62   The chain adjuster bolts
The four wheel nuts were used on the 1962–65 models only.

precisely the same amount (to keep the wheel alignment as it was originally) and retighten both locknuts. Retighten the spindle first from the right side, and then at the spindle nut on the left side. Before finally tightening the torque arm bolts on the earlier models with cable-operated brake, apply the brake to allow the cable to align itself properly. Securely tighten these bolts.

For 1966-9 models the method is similar except that the spindle head on the right side is released first and then the spindle nut on the left side. The reverse applies, of course, when reassembling. The reason for this is the different type of detachable wheel on these models, which have the brake drum on the left side.

Stretch of Chains. A chain may be considered to be worn out when its degree of stretch exceeds a quarter of an inch per foot length. To check, lay the chain in a straight line on a bench and close it up, i.e. shorten it as much as possible. Mark off a one-foot length, draw the chain out to its maximum length, and measure the distance between the two marks. The difference between the two measurements is the amount by which the chain has stretched. Alternatively, when the chain is closed up, mark off 50 pitches. If, when extended, this length covers 51 pitches the chain is due for replacement.

The Gearbox. The author does not advise the average B.S.A. owner to dismantle the gearbox and attempt major repairs himself. The work requires a considerable amount of skill and experience, and is best entrusted to an approved B.S.A. repair specialist. Fortunately gearbox trouble is rare and in the unlikely event of your needing to remove the gearbox assembly refer to the maker's *Workshop Manual*, obtainable through any B.S.A. dealer.

To Remove the Rear Wheel (General). All B.S.A. twins have quickly-detachable rear wheels but two different designs were used throughout the period covered by this booklet. This type of wheel simplifies a job which can be both awkward and dirty, because it means that the chain, sprocket, case, etc., are undisturbed when the wheel is taken out of the forks. When the spindle is refitted, keep its thread free from grit (this is specially important if a roadside tyre repair has been made) and give it a light coat of

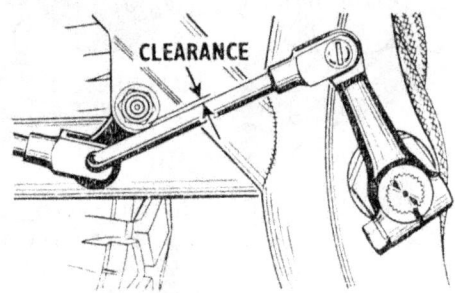

Fig 63   The two-piece brake rod (1962–5 Models)

The purpose of this design was to give smooth braking by making allowances for the different pivoting points of the swinging arm and the brake rod. The brake is in the "off" position.

grease. Be sure that the spindle head is firmly against the chain adjuster bolt after reassembly, otherwise the wheels will be out of alignment—a most important point.

To Remove the Rear Wheel (1962–6 Models) (*Right-side Brake*). The brake-plate, which carries the shoes, is on the right side of the wheel, and since the brake pedal is on the left side of the machine necessitates the use of a cross-over shaft. When this is to be withdrawn for lubrication purposes (*see* page 56) before removing the lever, scribe a line across the end face of the shaft and the lever, so that the two items can be reassembled in the correct relationship with each other. If you fail to do this, it is possible that you will refit the lever at an incorrect angle and so reduce your braking efficiency.

Early models of this period had cable brake operation but this was superseded by a hinged rod, both portions of which were coupled to a rocking lever mounted on the frame. The relative position of the short brake rod and lever are shown in Fig. 63.

GENERAL MAINTENANCE

To uncouple the connections on the cable-operated brake (Fig. 64), first unscrew the adjuster completely and remove the cable. Disconnect the torque link, and here note that the front end need be slackened only and that the split pin should not be removed (it is there to prevent accidental loss of the nut). At the rear end of the link remove the nut and, in order to allow sufficient space for release of the link, push the cable anchorage a little way into the brake plate. (The brake shoes will prevent it from falling inside.)

Similar instructions apply to the rod-operated brake (Fig. 64), but in

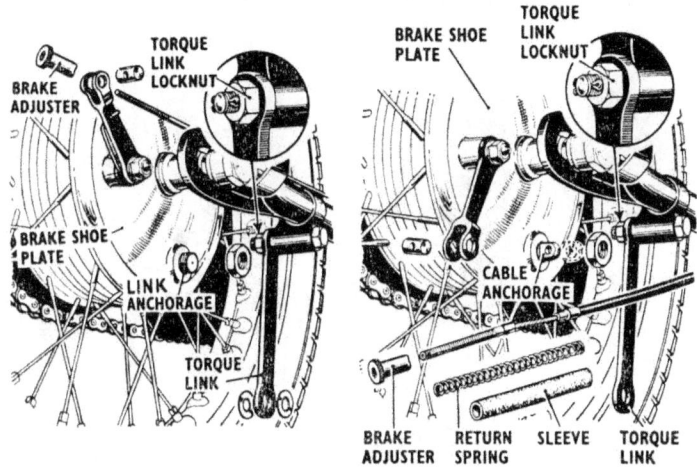

Fig 64   Removing the rear wheels (right-side brake)

On the cable-operated brake, before finally tightening the torque link anchorage nut on the cover plate apply the brake. This will allow the "eye" on the anchorage to turn slightly and the cable to align itself naturally.

this case after unscrewing the adjuster operate the brake pedal to draw the rod forward and out of the brake lever eye. The link anchorage at the brake merely requires removal of the nut to allow the link to be detached.

The wheel is attached to the chain sprocket by four nuts. Turn the rear wheel until each nut in succession is in a readily accessible position, engage first gear to lock the rear wheel, and unscrew the nuts. If a chaincase is fitted, it will be necessary to remove the rubber cap (just above the wheel spindle) and turn the wheel until the nuts are accessible, in succession, through the aperture. Unscrew the wheel spindle from the right side of the machine (turn anti-clockwise) and take out the spacing sleeve between the hub and swinging arm.

The wheel, complete with its brake plate, etc., can then be pulled away from the chain sprocket and lowered carefully to ground level. Do not disturb the spindle nut on the left side, because this retains the chain sprocket and its bearings and has no effect on wheel removal.

If the tyre is inflated, it will probably be necessary for you to adopt the following method for taking the wheel away. Stand beside the left side of your motor-cycle facing across the pillion seat and tilt the machine towards you, supporting its weight with the thighs. The right side will then be raised high enough to enable you to draw the wheel out on that side, past the mudguard. A punctured tyre will not cause the same difficulty with wheel removal.

When reassembling after mending a puncture it will be advisable to re-inflate the tyre *after* the wheel has been replaced. Before tightening the

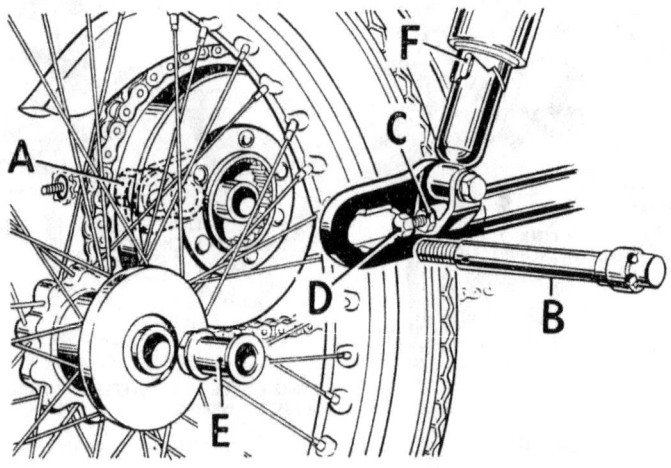

Fig 65   Removing the rear wheel (left-side brake)

On later models a shorter sleeve, E, was used when a speedometer drive unit was fitted, and in this case the cable connection must also be unscrewed.

cable anchorage nut, align the cable to give a straight pull at the brake lever. Readjust the brake as detailed on page 113.

To Remove the Rear Wheel (1965 *Lightning and Cyclone*, 1966–9 *Models*) (*Left-side Brake*). Since the brake drum and operating mechanism is on the left side of the machine, there is no necessity for a cross-over shaft and wheel removal is even simpler than on those machines with a right-side brake. Furthermore, wheel removal does not affect brake adjustment.

To remove the wheel (*see* Fig. 65), unscrew the spindle *B* from the right side, remove the spacing sleeve *E* and pull the wheel out of engagement with the splined drive in the brake drum. On models produced during the years

GENERAL MAINTENANCE 109

1966-9, it will also be necessary to disconnect the speedometer drive cable at the hub.

The nut *A* secures the brake drum, chainwheel, etc., and must not be disturbed except for purposes of chain adjustment (*see* page 104). A shorter mudguard with reduced valances greatly improves the ease with which the wheel can be removed, compared with earlier models.

Wheel Bearings. Ball journals are used in the front and rear wheels and adjustment is unnecessary. They are packed with grease during assembly and this will suffice until the hubs are dismantled for complete overhaul (say 12,000 miles).

Removing the Front Wheel (General). When you apply your brakes you will have noticed that your weight is thrown forward and obviously this phenomenon increases the pressure between the front tyre and the road. It follows that your front brake is the one with the greatest stopping power. B.S.A. engines have been giving a steadily increasing power output over the years, with a corresponding increase in road performance. To match this, the brakes have been improved by such features as increased diameter, increased lining width, two leading-shoes, etc. In all cases, when taking the wheel out of the forks check the brake linings and clean the drums of dust, etc. *Always* double check that the cable is securely attached to the lever with either a locknut or split-pin (according to the design) and that the fork end-caps are properly secured. *Remember—your life may depend on these precautions.* Adjust the brake in accordance with the instructions on page 113.

Removing the Front Wheel (1962-5 Models). Slacken the brake cable at the handlebar adjuster and remove the pin and locknut from the forked joint at the brake end of the cable. This will allow the cable to be slipped out of its anchorage on the cover plate (*see* Fig. 66).

It only remains to remove the fork leg end-caps and the wheel can be taken out. Support the wheel as the bolts are removed in order to save possible damage to the threads. Tighten the bolts evenly and securely in position. When replacing the wheel, note that a groove in the spindle determines the wheel position. Also—and this is a most important point—the slotted boss on the brake-shoe plate must engage with the tongue on the inside of the fork leg. This tongue prevents rotation of the plate when the brake is applied, and if not fitted as described the consequences can be serious.

Removing the Front Wheel (1965 *Lightning and Cyclone*, 1966-7 *Models, and* 1968 *Royal Star and Thunderbolt Models*). These models were fitted with a larger brake with the drum on the right side of the fork (Fig. 67), and removal is simple. Slacken the cable at its adjuster *F* on the brake cover plate and turn the lever on the plate by hand to increase still further the cable slackness, until the cable can be slipped through the slot in the forked joint *E* (without any need to remove the hinge pin). A torque arm is used to retain the cover plate and its nut *C* must be removed and the

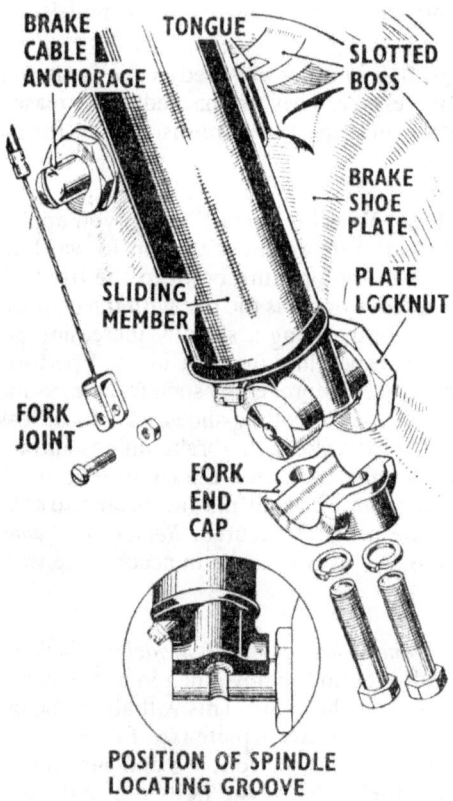

Fig 66   Removing the front wheel (1962–5 Models)

Note that the slot in the cable anchorage must be positioned to give a straight cable. Check that the plate locknut is quite tight before the wheel is replaced.

nuts at *D* slackened, to provide sufficient freedom of movement of the torque arm and allow the wheel to be taken out.

Next, release the clamp bolt *A* and unscrew the spindle *B*, supporting the wheel while this is being done. This spindle has a *left-hand thread* and must be turned in a *clockwise* direction to unscrew.

Take care in handling the wheel because, although the sleeve which projects from the brake side of the hub is a press fit in the hub, it may, if

GENERAL MAINTENANCE 111

hit hard enough, be forced into the hub interior. In this event, the spindle should be used to recover and reposition the sleeve in the hub.

When the wheel is being replaced and is loosely in position, refit the torque arm, but do not tighten its nuts. As the spindle B is being tightened, it has a tendency to draw the fork legs together, and if this occurs they will

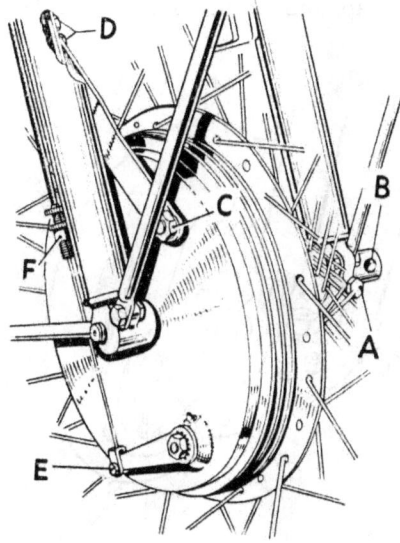

Fig 67 Removing the front wheel (1965 Lightning and Cyclone, 1966–67 Models, 1968 Royal Star and Thunderbolt)

Note the cable adjuster on the brake plate. A second adjuster is on the handlebar lever.

no longer slide freely. As soon as the spindle is tightly in position, stand astride the machine, grasp the handlebars, and "pump" the forks up and down several times to allow the left fork leg to align itself on the spindle. When you are satisfied that the fork legs are functioning correctly, securely tighten the clamp bolt A. Now tighten the torque arm nuts C and D.

Removing the Front Wheel (1968—*except Royal Star and Thunderbolt— and* 1969). Two leading-shoe brakes are fitted to these models, giving the ultimate in braking performance. Removal of the wheel begins with the slackening of the brake cable at its handlebar adjuster, followed by the disconnection of the cable forked joint from its brake lever at E (Fig. 68). On earlier models, a spring clip pivot pin was used but this was eventually replaced by a pivot pin with locknut. Next, remove the fork leg end-caps and the wheel can be taken out. Support the wheel as the bolts are removed, in order to save possible damage to the threads.

When replacing the wheel note that a groove in the spindle determines the wheel position. Tighten the bolts evenly and securely in position.

Two most important assembly points must be observed. First, the slotted boss on the brake-shoe plate must engage with the tongue on the inside of the fork leg and, secondly, the fork leg end-caps are not identical and must not be mixed up. On some models, letters or figures were stamped on the fork leg and on the cap, and on others drill-point holes were made. The

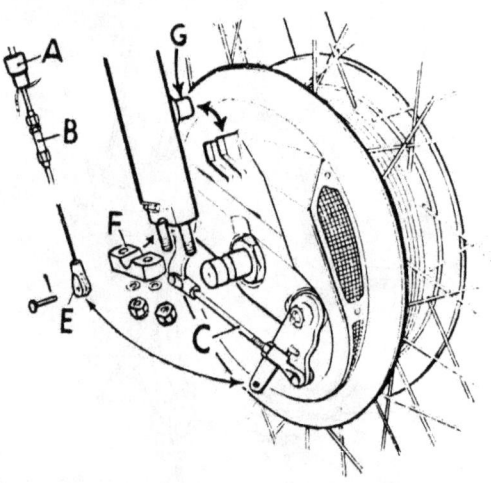

Fig 68 The two leading-shoe brake fitted to 1968 (except Royal Star and Thunderbolt) and 1969 Models

The main cable adjuster is at B. The stop-light switch A was introduced on 1969 models. On some models the first pin at E took the form of a spring clip and pivot combined.

caps must be assembled with the identification mark adjacent to the corresponding mark on the fork leg.

If the first important assembly detail is not properly carried out the brake will be defective and the consequences could be serious. If the second is overlooked, the steering will be adversely effected.

Checking Wheel Alignment. Following any adjustment to the rear chain it is always advisable to check the alignment of the wheels. As already mentioned in the section "Rear Chain Adjustment" (page 104), if the adjusters have been moved by exactly the same amount, then the alignment should be correct (always assuming that it was correct before the adjustment).

If your tyres are of the same section (i.e. width), then a piece of string can be drawn tightly across the side walls of the two tyres at a point just below the silencers. Keep the steering in the straight-ahead position when,

GENERAL MAINTENANCE 113

if the wheels are in correct alignment, the string will contact the tyre walls at two places on each wheel. This is one of those jobs which is greatly simplified if you have an assistant to hold one end of the string.

Where tyre sizes are different, it will be preferable to make a straight edge, such as a plank of wood with one edge "stepped" to correspond with the difference in tyre section and a piece cut out to clear the central stand. As before the straight edge must touch both tyre walls at two points.

A good guide to accurate wheel alignment is given by the feel of the steering. If a solo machine has a tendency to pull one way or the other when riding on a straight road, the first suspect is that of wheel alignment (although, of course, there may be other reasons).

It is impossible to make any adjustment to the front wheel for the purpose of realigning the wheels should this be found necessary, and the rear wheel must be aligned to the front wheel. If the chain adjustment is correct, only the right-side wheel adjuster need be moved in order to bring the wheels into line, but if chain setting is also required, then adjusters on both sides of the wheel will need attention (*see* "Rear Chain Adjustment," page 104).

Brake Adjustment (General). Brakes must always be kept at a state of maximum efficiency; too often is this vital equipment sadly neglected. *Whenever the movement of the hand lever or foot pedal has become excessive, adjust the brake!* The best method is also the simplest. Adjust the brake until the shoes just rub on the drum and then slacken off by one or two turns on the adjuster. By this means, the shoes should be just clear of the drum when the brake is not in use, but close enough for immediate contact when the brake is applied. Do not make the adjustment too close, however, because the heat generated by constant rubbing of the lining on the drum will reduce braking efficiency and road performance, and also be liable to melt the grease in the hub.

A good guide to the state of efficiency of your brakes is whether, when the brake is applied, the angle between the rod (or cable) and the lever on the brake-plate exceeds 90 degrees; if it does it is time to consider renewal of the brake linings.

Front Brake Adjustment. The front brakes on all B.S.A. Twins are adjusted at the handlebar lever by means of the knurled screw at that end of the cable, but some models have an additional (main) adjuster in the form of a screwed sleeve with a knurled locking ring, located at the cable abutment on the brake shoe plate. With these models it is also possible to reposition the brake cam lever on a different serration or to turn it over, to give still further brake adjustment.

The main adjuster for the two leading shoe brakes fitted to some 1968 models and all 1969 models is to be found midway in the cable.

On these models only, when the shoes are replaced it will be necessary to "balance" them in order to equalize their braking effort and this is carried out after the wheel is replaced in position. Disconnect the tie-rod C (Fig. 68), between the brake levers of the brake-plate mechanism, by taking out the pivot pins at each end, and slacken the locknut.

Apply the brake, and keep it applied by means of a strong rubber band wrapped round the handlebar lever, which will leave your hands free for the remainder of the adjustment. Turn the short (rearmost) lever in its normal direction of travel by means of a spanner applied to the spindle nut, until the brake shoe is firmly in contact with the brake drum.

Then adjust the length of the tie-rod until the pivot pins at both ends of the rod can just be inserted, when both shoes will be in contact with the brake drum and at the same pressure. Fit new split-pins to the pivots (or spring pivots as the case may be) and retighten the locknut.

Rear Brake Adjustment. The rear brake on all models, whether cable- or rod-operated, is adjusted at the lever on the brake plate (Fig. 69). It is a

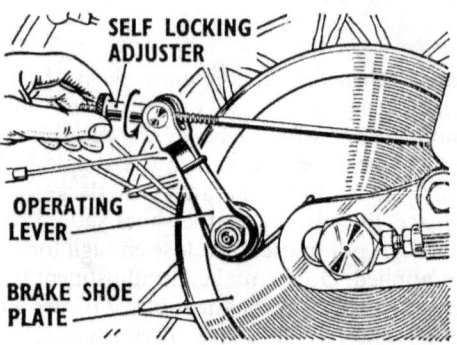

Fig 69 Adjustment of the rear brake
The principle is the same for left or right side brakes.

simple matter of screwing up the adjuster, which in the majority of cases is a knurled sleeve, but in others a wing nut is used.

Brake Linings. The life of the linings will vary considerably, depending upon the conditions of usage, but inevitably the time will come when the linings require renewal. After the wheel has been taken out of the forks (*see* pages 106 and 109), remove the cover plate and examine the linings If they are worn down to the rivet heads it is time they were replaced.

The shoes are retained by strong springs and it will be necessary to prise the shoes apart before the springs can be removed. A word of warning here—the springs are strong enough to cause damage to your fingers if carelessly handled. The easiest way to remove the shoes is to lever them

GENERAL MAINTENANCE

upwards and inwards off the cams and fulcrum pins in the *reverse* manner to that shown in Fig. 70.

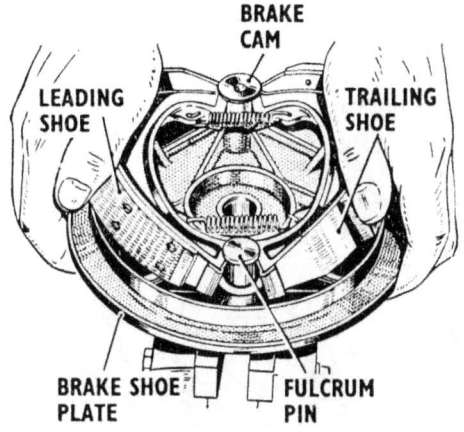

Fig 70   Replacing the brake shoes

The shoes and springs are assembled before fitting to the brake plate and the method shown avoids trapping the fingers.

Relining the shoes is not a job for the amateur because, unless the riveting is skilfully completed, the result may be a "spongy" brake action. Far better to take the shoes to a B.S.A. dealer and exchange them for a replacement pair or, if these are not available, to have them relined by a skilled mechanic. Alternatively, most of the large brake lining manufacturers operate a relining service and their nearest branch should be contacted.

Refitting the shoes to the cover plate is shown in the illustration (Fig. 70), when, with the springs in position and the shoes located on the brake cam and fulcrum pin, the shoes should be pressed downwards and outwards with the palms of the hands. They will then "snap" into position.

1962–5 *Models, Except Lightning and Cyclone.* On these models, with full-width hubs, the cover plate on the front wheel is released after unscrewing the large spindle nut next to the plate. These shoes, and those in the rear hub, are of the floating type and the linings are not symmetrical with the shoes. *It is most important that the shoes are fitted correctly (see* Fig. 71), otherwise braking may be dangerously fierce.

When new shoes have been fitted they should be centralized in the drum and this can be done after the complete wheel has been replaced in position. Slacken the fulcrum pin nut and apply the brake, when the pin will take up a new position in the brake plate and the shoes will be symmetrical with the brake drum. Be sure to tighten the fulcrum pin nut.

1969 *Models and Some* 1968 *Models.* The front cover plate on the two leading-shoe brake fitted to these models requires the large spindle nut next to the cover plate to be removed before the plate can be released.

Steering Head Adjustment (All Models Except 1969). Do not allow the steering head bearings to be out of adjustment because if the clearances are too great the ball tracks may become indented due to road shocks, making accurate adjustment impossible and the races will have to be renewed.

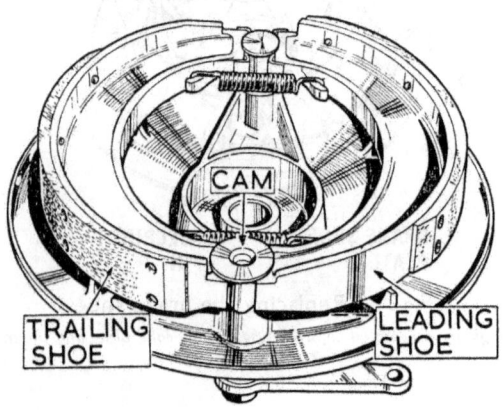

Fig 71   Fully floating brake shoes (1962–5 Models, except Lightning and Cyclone)

The relationship of the linings, shoes, and cam can be clearly seen. Do not depart from this arrangement in any circumstances.

To check, place a support below the crankcase so that the front wheel is clear of the ground, grasp the forks in the manner shown in Fig. 72 and try to rock them backwards and forwards. Any play which can be felt at the steering head means that attention is necessary, but do not confuse this with the small amount of play present at the bottom of the fork legs and which is the normal working clearance.

On 1962–5 models with a headlamp nacelle, it will be necessary to unscrew the steering damper knob and its rod, and to unscrew the rim of the anti-theft lock, to allow the fork cover to be lifted off and expose the cap-nut.

The method of adjustment is the same for all models. Release the clamping bolts on the fork legs below the lamp or housing (according to model) and then the clip bolt below the handlebars. Remove the cap-nut at the head of the steering column, to expose the slotted adjusting sleeve (Fig. 73).

Tighten the sleeve a little at a time until there is an absolute minimum of play in the head bearings, but *the adjustment must not be made too close.* This can be verified by holding the bars lightly and swinging them to left

GENERAL MAINTENANCE 117

and to right slowly, when the steering must be quite free and turn smoothly. Firmly tighten the handlebar clip bolt and the two fork leg clamp bolts.

1969 *Models*. Adjustment of the steering head for these models is made in precisely the same manner as for the above machines, except that the slotted adjustment sleeve is no longer fitted and the cap-nut alone serves as an adjuster.

Dismantling the Front Forks. Complete dismantling of the front forks for renewal of the bearing sleeves is a task which requires the use of

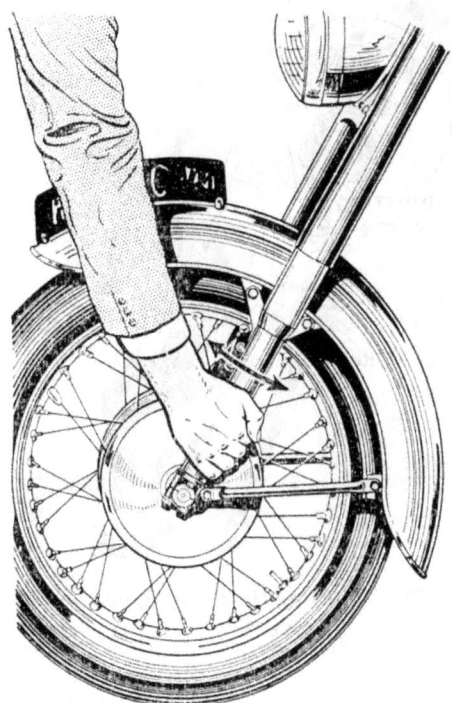

Fig 72   Testing the steering head for bearing slackness

several B.S.A. Service Tools. The combined cost of these is such that for the rare occasions on which this repair is necessary it is preferable for the work to be undertaken by a B.S.A. Service dealer, who has the proper equipment and the skill to do a good job for you. If, however, you are determined to strip the forks yourself, then the author advises you to follow the instructions given in the *B.S.A. Workshop Manual.*

Changing the Fork Springs. In the event of a broken fork spring, or the need to change them for another pair of stronger (or weaker) springs, the fork legs will have to be removed from the machine as individual units, for which purpose one B.S.A. Service Tool is required, No. 61-3350. In emergency, even this can be dispensed with and the fork leg cap-nut used

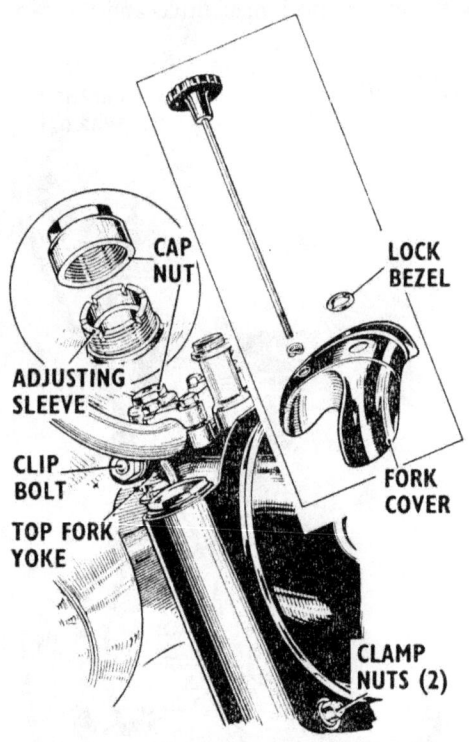

Fig 73 Adjusting the steering head bearings

The illustration shows the steering head assembly for earlier models with a headlamp nacelle. The principle of adjustment is the same for all models.

instead, although it may be damaged in the process (see later in this section).

First, remove the front wheel as explained on pages 109 and 110, and then the mudguard and stays.

On 1962–5 models which carry the headlamp in a nacelle, unscrew the steering damper and rod, the rim of the anti-theft lock, and then the top yoke cover.

On later models, with twin speedometer and rev-counter heads mounted on a platform on the top yoke, pull out the lighting bulbs (their holders are a "spring" fit) and disconnect the driving cables at the base of the

GENERAL MAINTENANCE 119

instruments. This will allow the platform and instruments to be lifted off as a unit. On yet other models, where the fork legs have rubber gaiters, slacken the clip (where fitted) and slide the gaiter downwards off the cover.

Remove the fork cap nuts. 1966–8 models only, were fitted with a special damper rod attached to these nuts and the rod must be released and allowed to drop down inside the main fork leg.

Now take Service Tool No. 61-3350 (or 61-3824 for 1969 models) and screw it into the top of the leg, without using the large washer and nut. (This is a multi-service tool and some threads are for use on other models.) Slacken, but do not remove the fork leg clamp bolt, because this bolt will retain the cover, headlamp, etc., while the fork leg is out of the machine.

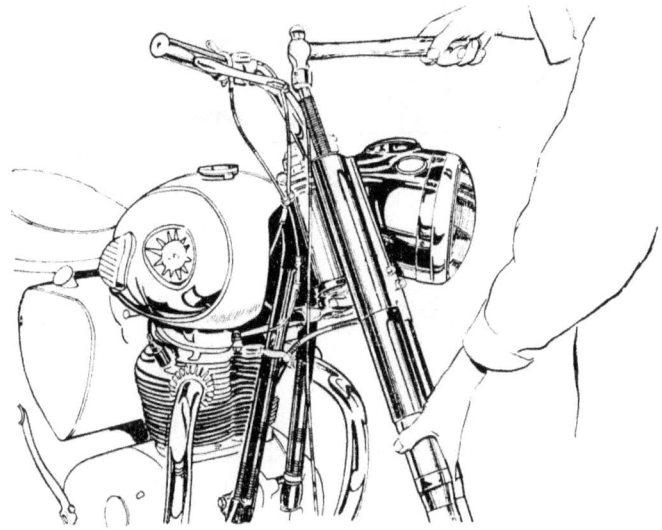

Fig 74 Removal of the fork leg from the yokes

Service tool No. 61-3350 or 61-3824 (depending on the model, see text) is shown in position in the top of the fork leg.

Grasp the lower end of the fork leg and strike a sharp blow with a mallet on the top of the service tool, which will have the effect of extracting the tapered end of the main fork shaft from its socket in the top yoke Fig. 74). The fork leg can be drawn out downwards as a complete assembly and the process repeated for the other leg.

All that remains is for the springs to be lifted off. Replacement springs should be liberally coated with grease before fitting.

Replacing the Fork Legs. Service tool No. 61-3350 (or 61-3824 for 1969 models only), is now used for assembly purposes. Screw the tool into the top of the fork leg (without, of course, using the large collar and nut) and slide the whole assembly up through the bottom fork yoke and into the top yoke. Add the collar and nut and tighten the latter until the leg is firmly engaged with its taper seat in the top yoke. The method is shown in the illustration (Fig. 75). *Before the tool is removed, tighten the leg clamping bolt.*

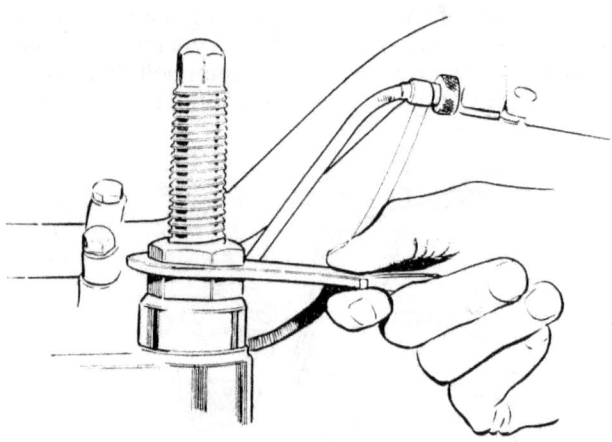

Fig 75   Using Service Tool No. 61-3350 or 61-3824 (depending on the model, see text) to replace the fork leg

On 1966-8 models only, the damper rod must now be retrieved from inside the fork leg and screwed back into the cap-nut. A piece of internally threaded tubing about 9 in. long will be useful at this juncture. (Thread size 5/16 in. dia. × 26 T.P.I. × 1/2 in. long). The cap-nut can still be raised sufficiently for oil to be added.

Fit the other fork leg in the same manner and add 1/3 pint of a lubricating oil such as Castrolite (or its equivalent in other brands—*see* "Correct Lubrication," page 52). Replace the cap-nuts, temporarily slacken the leg clamping bolts, and tighten the nuts firmly, afterwards retightening the clamp bolts.

The remainder of the assembly is a straightforward matter of replacing the parts and does not call for any special comment.

Rear Suspension. The dampers are self-contained units comprising a compression spring adjustable for load, and a sealed hydraulic damping device. It is not possible to dismantle the whole unit but two adjustments can be made by the private owner.

A spiral cam is incorporated in each unit to accommodate variations in load, such as the addition of a pillion passenger, and can be set in any

GENERAL MAINTENANCE 121

one of three positions (Fig. 76). A special "C" spanner is required for this adjustment and is included in the tool-kit of a new machine.

It is possible to change the springs and for this purpose the damper units must be removed from the machine one at a time, otherwise there will not be any support for the rear of the frame. Because the springs are

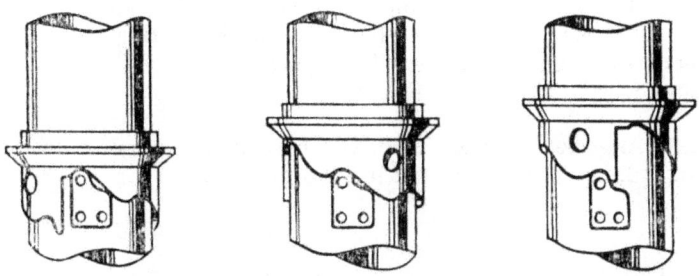

Fig 76   The Girling hydraulic suspension unit adjustment

On the left is shown the first position for a light load, in the centre the second position for a medium load, and on the right the third position for a heavy load.

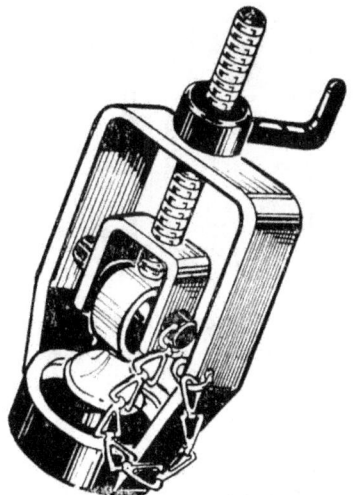

Fig 77   The B.S.A. Service tool 61-3503 shown in action

so strong, B.S.A. Service Tool No. 61-3503 is a necessity, and this enables the spring to be compressed and retained in that position while the semi-circular collets are removed (Fig. 77). Unscrewing the tool afterwards allows the spring to extend until it can be lifted out. The cam loading should be set to the lightest loading position before attempting to extract the spring.

Note: new (stronger) springs are always advisable when a change is being made from solo to sidecar purposes.

Tyre Pressures. These will vary according to machine weight and tyre size, but an all-round figure of 21 p.s.i. for the front wheel and 22 p.s.i. for the rear wheel should be satisfactory for normal roads and moderate speeds. When a pillion rider and/or luggage is added, you should determine the precise weight on each wheel (a public weighbridge can be of some assistance here) and obtain revised tyre pressures from a Dunlop Tyre and Pressure Schedule kept by most garages.

Wheel Alignment (Sidecar Outfits). The manufacturers do not provide built-in sidecar connections and it is normal practice for the proprietary

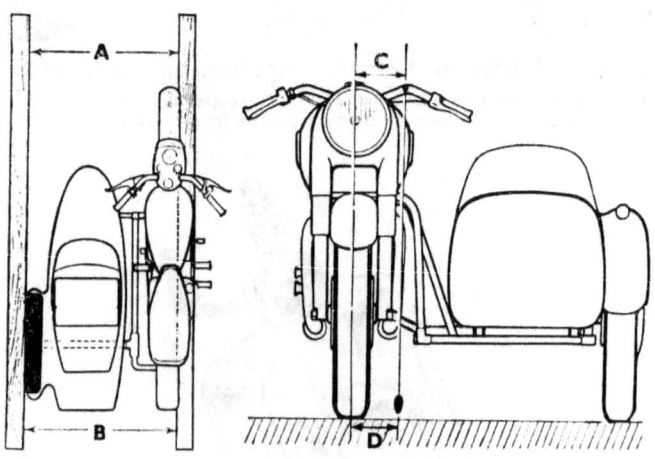

Fig 78   Correct sidecar alignment

The "toe-in" is the difference between the dimension A and B with A the smaller of the two distances the "lean-out" is the difference between dimension C and D with C the greater of the two distances.

sidecar makers to supply their own methods of attaching their wares to different motor-cycles. Their couplings are always adjustable within limits, to allow correct alignment of all three wheels, both horizontally and vertically.

Correct alignment is essential for precise steering and for avoiding a continuous "pull" to one side of the road, a fault which can be extremely tiring on a long run. Misalignment will also cause excessive and rapid tyre wear and for these reasons it is worth while spending time and trouble in etting perfect alignment.

GENERAL MAINTENANCE

First of all, check the wheel alignment of the solo machine, because it will be of little use to try to align a third wheel to two wheels which themselves may be out of line (*see* "Checking Wheel Alignment," page 112).

Two straight edges are required and these can be in the form of planks of wood, not less than 9 feet long.

Find a level piece of flat ground (such as a concrete yard) and place the edges alongside the wheels, as shown in Fig 78. If the front tyre is smaller in section than the rear one—as is usual on modern B.S.A. twins—there will be a gap between the straight edge and the front tyre corresponding to half the difference in the widths of the front and rear tyres. The gap must be consistent across the front wheel and, of course, will be so if the solo wheel alignment is correct.

The dimension A just in front of the front wheel, should be less than that at B just behind the rear wheel, by between 1/2 in. and 3/4 in. This is known as "toe-in."

Vertical alignment is equally important. Tie a plumb-line to the right handlebar and measure the distances C and D. In this case, dimension C should be one inch greater than dimension D.

The upper sidecar connections are normally the ones to be adjusted to obtain these conditions, but this advice may be different according to the individual sidecar manufacturer's design of couplings.

When Attaching a Sidecar. The addition of a sidecar creates a different set of conditions compared with a solo machine, requiring a completely new driving technique and modifications to the machine to accommodate the additional load and other factors.

Fit new front fork springs of a greater "poundage" (*see* "Changing the Fork Springs," page 118) and also new and stronger rear suspension springs (*see* "Rear Suspension," page 120). These will take care of the additional weight.

Lower the gear ratios. A new gearbox sprocket of two teeth less than that fitted for solo use will be sufficient for a single-seat sidecar. It is accessible through the primary chaincase after removing the clutch (*see* "Dismantling the Clutch," page 101). You must be prepared for a corresponding loss in maximum speed and general all-round performance.

A further item is that of the front tyre. A ribbed tread is used on the front wheel of most B.S.A. twins and this should be changed for one of the studded type. This tyre will give better road-holding and braking.

Index

ALIGNMENT—
  sidecar, 122
  solo, 112
Amal carburettor, 24
  adjustments, 25
  jet table, 31
Automatic ignition advance, 48

BATTERY, topping up, 61
Brakes adjustment, 113

CARBURETTOR adjustment, 25, 28
Chains—
  adjustment, front, 95
  adjustment, rear, 104
  lubrication, front, 52
  lubrication, rear, 53
Clutch—
  control adjustment, 95
  dismantling, 101
  spring pressure, 98
Contact-breaker gap, 70
Controls, 6
Cylinder block
  removal, 85
  replacing, 90
Cylinder head—
  gasket, 80
  removal, 79
  replacing, 91

DECARBONIZING, 77

ELECTRICAL maintenance, 60

FILTERS—
  air, 37
  oil, 42, 44
Front forks—
  dismantling, 117
  draining, 54

GEARBOX—
  draining, 51
  lubrication, 51

HEADLAMP bulbs, 60

LUBRICATION—
  brake controls, 55
  contact-breaker, 48
  chart, 49
  engine, 39
  front forks, 54
  gearbox, 50
  handlebar controls, 57
  primary chain, 52
  secondary chain, 53
  steering head, 53
  wheel bearings, 55

OIL—
  pressure control valve, 46
  pump ball valve, 46

PISTON—
  removal, 87
  replacing, 89
  rings, 88

REAR suspension, 120

SPARKING plugs—
  cleaning, 67
  gap, 67
Starting, emergency, 16
Steering head—
  adjustment, 116
  lubrication, 53

TIMING—
  ignition, 71
  valve, 93

VALVE—
  clearances, 76
  guides, 82
  springs, 82
Valves, grinding-in, 84

WHEEL—
  removal, front, 109
  removal, rear, 106

OTHER MOTORCYCLE MANUALS AVAILABLE IN THIS SERIES

AJS (BOOK OF) ALL MODELS 1955-1965:
350cc & 500cc Singles ~ Models 16, 16S, 18, 18S

ARIEL WORKSHOP MANUAL 1933-1951:
All single, twin & 4 cylinder models

ARIEL (BOOK OF) MAINTENANCE & REPAIR MANUAL 1932-1939:
LF3, LF4, LG, NF3, NF4, NG, OG, VA, VA3, VA4, VB, VF3, VF4, VG, Red Hunter LH, NH, OH, VH & Square Four 4F, 4G, 4H

BMW FACTORY WORKSHOP MANUAL R27, R28:
English, German, French and Spanish text

BMW FACTORY WORKSHOP MANUAL R50, R50S, R60, R69S:
Also includes a supplement for the USA models: R50US, R60US, R69US.
English, German, French and Spanish text

BSA PRE-WAR SINGLES & TWINS (BOOK OF) 1936-1939:
All Pre-War single & twin cylinder SV & OHV models through 1939
150cc, 250cc, 350cc, 500cc, 600cc, 750cc & 1,000cc

BSA SINGLES (BOOK OF) 1945-1954:
OHV & SV 250cc, 350cc, 500cc & 600cc, Groups B, C & M

BSA SINGLES (BOOK OF) 1955-1967:
B31, B32, B33, B34 and "Star" B40 & SS90

BSA 250cc SINGLES (BOOK OF) 1954-1970:
B31, B32, B33, B34 and "Star" B40 & SS90

BSA TWINS (BOOK OF) 1948-1962:
All 650cc & 500cc twins

BSA TWINS (SECOND BOOK OF) 1962-1969:
All 650cc & 500cc, A50 & A65 OHV unit construction twins

DUCATI OHC FACTORY WORKSHOP MANUAL:
160 Junior Monza, 250 Monza, 250 GT, 250 Mark 3, 250 Mach 1, 250 SCR & 350 Sebring

HONDA 250 & 305cc FACTORY WORKSHOP MANUAL:
C.72 C.77 CS.72, CS.77, CB.72, CB.77 [HAWK]

HONDA 125 & 150cc FACTORY WORKSHOP MANUAL:
C.92, CS.92, CB.92, C.95 & CA.95

HONDA 90 (BOOK OF) ALL MODELS UP TO 1966:
All 90cc variations including the S90, CM90, C200, S65, Trail 90 & C65 models

HONDA 50cc FACTORY WORKSHOP MANUAL: C.100

HONDA 50cc FACTORY WORKSHOP MANUAL: C.110

HONDA (BOOK OF) MAINTENANCE & REPAIR 1960-1966:
50cc C.100, C.102, C.110 & C.114 ~ 125cc C.92 & CB.92
250cc C.72 & CB.72 ~ 305cc CB.77

LAMBRETTA (BOOK OF) MAINTENANCE & REPAIR:
125 & 150cc, all models up to 1958, except model "48".

NORTON FACTORY TWIN CYLINDER WORKSHOP MANUAL 1957-1970: *Lightweight Twins:* 250cc Jubilee, 350cc Navigator and 400cc Electra and the *Heavyweight Twins:* Model 77, 88, 88SS, 99, 99SS, Sports Special, Manxman, Mercury, Atlas, G15, P11, N15, Ranger (P11A).

NORTON (BOOK OF) MAINTENANCE & REPAIR 1932-1939:
All Pre-War SV, OHV and OHC models: 16H, 16I, 18, 19, 20, 50, 55, ES2, CJ, CSI, International 30 & 40

SUZUKI 200 & 250cc FACTORY WORKSHOP MANUAL:
250cc T20 [X-6 Hustler] ~ 200cc T200 [X-5 Invader & Sting Ray Scrambler]

SUZUKI 250cc FACTORY WORKSHOP MANUAL: 250cc ~ T10

TRIUMPH (BOOK OF) MAINTENANCE & REPAIR 1935-1939:
All Pre-War single & twin cylinder models: L2/1, 2/1, 2/5, 3/1, 3/2, 3/5, 5/1, 5/2, 5/3, 5/4, 5/5, 5/10, 6/1, Tiger 70, 80, 90 & 2H. Tiger 70C, 3S & 3H, Tiger 80C & 5H, Tiger 90C, 6S, 2HC & 3SC, 5T & 5S and T100

TRIUMPH 1937-1951 WORKSHOP MANUAL (A. St. J. Masters):
Covers rigid frame and sprung hub single cylinder SV & OHV and twin cylinder OHV pre-war, military, and post-war models

TRIUMPH 1945-1955 FACTORY WORKSHOP MANUAL NO.11:
Covers pre-unit, twin-cylinder rigid frame, sprung hub, swing-arm and 350cc, 500cc & 650cc.

VELOCETTE (BOOK OF) MAINTENANCE & REPAIR:
Covers LE Mk. I, II, & III, Valiant, Vogue, MOV, MAC, KSS, KTS, Viper, Venom & Thruxton. Includes some limited material on the Viceory scooter

VESPA (BOOK OF) MAINTENANCE & REPAIR 1946-1959:
All 125cc & 150cc models including 42/L2 & Gran Sport

VINCENT WORKSHOP MANUAL 1935-1955:
All Series A, B & C Models

www.VelocePress.com

www.ingramcontent.com/pod-product-compliance
Lightning Source LLC
Chambersburg PA
CBHW070555170426
43201CB00012B/1850